Combating Student Plagiarism

CHANDOS
INFORMATION PROFESSIONAL SERIES

Series Editor: Ruth Rikowski
(email: Rikowskigr@aol.com)

Chandos' new series of books are aimed at the busy information professional. They have been specially commissioned to provide the reader with an authoritative view of current thinking. They are designed to provide easy-to-read and (most importantly) practical coverage of topics that are of interest to librarians and other information professionals. If you would like a full listing of current and forthcoming titles, please visit our website www.chandospublishing.com or contact Hannah Grace-Williams on email info@chandospublishing.com or telephone number +44 (0) 1993 848726.

New authors: we are always pleased to receive ideas for new titles; if you would like to write a book for Chandos, please contact Dr Glyn Jones on email gjones@chandospublishing.com or telephone number +44 (0) 1993 848726.

Bulk orders: some organisations buy a number of copies of our books. If you are interested in doing this, we would be pleased to discuss a discount. Please contact Hannah Grace-Williams on email info@chandospublishing.com or telephone number +44 (0) 1993 848726.

Combating Student Plagiarism: An academic librarian's guide

LYNN D. LAMPERT

Chandos Publishing
Oxford · England

Chandos Publishing (Oxford) Limited
TBAC Business Centre
Avenue 4
Station Lane
Witney
Oxford OX28 4BN
UK
Tel: +44 (0) 1993 848726 Fax: +44 (0) 1865 884448
Email: info@chandospublishing.com
www.chandospublishing.com

First published in Great Britain in 2008

ISBN:
978 1 84334 282 3 (paperback)
978 1 84334 283 0 (hardback)
1 84334 282 0 (paperback)
1 84334 283 9 (hardback)

British Library Cataloguing-in-Publication Data.
A catalogue record for this book is available from the British Library.

Typeset by Avocet Typeset, Chilton, Aylesbury, Bucks.
Printed in the UK and USA.

To my husband Andy, our daughter Rebecca,
and the rest of our pack

Contents

List of figures and tables

Figures

Tables

About the author

Lynn D. Lampert, a native of Los Angeles, continues to live in southern California. She is currently the chair of reference and instructional services and coordinator of information literacy at California State University Northridge (CSUN). Before joining the faculty at CSUN in 2001, Lynn worked as a reference and instruction librarian at California Lutheran University in Thousand Oaks, California.

Lynn earned both a master's in library and information science and a master's in history from the University of California, Los Angeles, in 1998. She received her BA degree in history from the University of California, Santa Barbara.

Lynn is an active member of the Association of College and Research Libraries (a division of the American Library Association) and several other regional and national professional library associations. She has authored many publications, appearing both within and outside the field of library and information science, focusing on information literacy, the role of the library and librarians in combating student plagiarism and other important issues facing academic librarianship. Lynn frequently presents on critical issues in information literacy and instructional programming, and other public service issues facing academic libraries.

Lynn can be contacted at lynn.lampert@csun.edu.

Acknowledgements

Many people have shaped and contributed to my knowledge of information literacy and academic librarianship. Writing this book would not have been possible without certain mentors and colleagues encouraging me to continue to write and conduct research about the roles that academic librarians can play in combating student plagiarism and thereby increasing student information literacy skills.

I first became interested in the topic of student plagiarism and its connection to information literacy programming in spring 2003. At that time I was working with journalism students at my library at California State University Northridge. Simultaneously the plagiarism scandal involving the reporter Jayson Blair that rocked the *New York Times* hit the news, and led me to focus my dialogues with journalism faculty on the issues of student plagiarism, information literacy and information ethics. I was encouraged to conduct research in this area by Professor Linda Bowen and other journalism faculty members.

From the research I conducted through partnerships with the journalism faculty, I went on to develop a poster session and write a paper which I presented at the 2004 LOEX of the West Conference in Boise, Idaho. This paper was published later in 2004 as an article ('Integrating discipline-based anti-plagiarism instruction into the information literacy curriculum', *Reference Services Review*, 32(4): 331, 347–55).

In late 2005 the Association of College and Research Libraries (ACRL), a division of the American Library Association (ALA), contacted me to ask if I would conduct an in-person pre-conference on the role of the academic librarian in combating student plagiarism for the 2006 ALA Annual Midwinter Meeting in San Antonio, Texas. The pre-conference was a success, leading to many fruitful discussions with participants long after the program was over. After that 2006 pre-conference, the ACRL went on to invite me to create an online webcast which is now entitled *The Role of the Librarian in Combating Student Plagiarism*. This 1.5-hour-long program has been delivered many times to participants across the USA and around the world. I would like to thank the ACRL for its support of my research and for providing me with a platform to discuss this important professional issue with other librarians. In particular, I would like to thank Stephanie Orphan and Margot Sutton Conahan of the ACRL and Hope Kandel of Learning Times for their support of these projects. I have learned a great deal from these experiences.

In 2007 I was invited by the University of Northern Iowa to conduct two half-day workshops on the issue of plagiarism, sponsored by various colleges, the provost and the Rod Library. In developing these talks and the assessment instruments that were utilized to query students about student plagiarism issues, I learned a great deal more about how academic librarians, faculty and students view the issues of plagiarism and information ethics. I would like to thank the faculty and staff of the Rod Library and UNI for their generous support of my research, travel and talks. Special thanks go to the dean, Marilyn Mercado, and librarian Sandra Warner for making my visit to Cedar Falls,

Iowa, both memorable and rewarding.

Beyond my involvement with the ACRL in raising awareness about the linkages that can exist between student plagiarism and the information literacy instructional programming that librarians and libraries are responsible for, I have also been fortunate to have many colleagues who have supported my work on this and other information literacy issues. I would like to extend my sincerest thanks to several wonderful friends and colleagues whose support and encouragement have always managed to keep me moving forward: Stephanie Brasley, Susan Curzon, Katherine Dabbour, Esther Grassian and Joan Kaplowitz.

In addition, I would be remiss if I did not thank and acknowledge my colleagues and co-workers at California State University Northridge (CSUN) and the information literacy coordinators within the California State University (CSU) library system, who have always been very receptive to investigating and developing innovative strategies that help us to infuse information literacy into the curriculum and culture of the campus. I would also like especially to thank the staff of the Interlibrary Loan Office at the Oviatt Library at CSUN for all their help in obtaining resources that existed beyond our collection.

After reviewing my 2004 LOEX of the West paper on discipline-based approaches to combating student plagiarism, the late Dr Ilene F. Rockman, who was both a close mentor and colleague, encouraged me to do more with my research by thoroughly studying the instructional role that librarians could play in the area of student plagiarism. A colleague from the CSU library system and a passionate advocate for applied research in the field of information literacy, Ilene's interest in my work and ideas continues to inspire my studies in the area of student plagiarism and information literacy. I will always be grateful for the tremendous support and mentorship she offered.

In terms of the preparation of this book, I would like to thank Chandos Publishing and my editor Glyn Jones for the patience and wonderful support they have provided. Many thanks to Cherry Ekins for her meticulous copyediting and much-needed support via e-mail. I also would like to acknowledge those entities and people who have allowed me permission to reprint images in this publication: the Los Angeles Chapter of the Boy Scouts of America (Figure I.1) and Barbara Fister and the ACRL (Figure 2.1).

Beyond my home institution and the circle of colleagues and friends I have met through my work in librarianship, I would like to thank my family for their support for my research and writing. My thanks to my husband, Andrew Diekmann, who has been supportive of me writing this book – especially during a period when we have also been expecting the birth of our first child, Rebecca. I would also like to acknowledge my mother, Frances Lampert – who has throughout my life always encouraged me and my sister, Lisa Lampert-Weissig.

Those who know me well will not be surprised to learn that I lastly feel compelled to credit my two beagles, Daisy and Gatsby, with my ability to finish this book. After all, they lay dutifully by my feet as I sat at my laptop for very long stretches writing the text. Supportive friends like that are hard to come by.

List of acronyms

ABET	Accreditation Board for Engineering and Technology
ACRL	Association of College and Research Libraries
ALA	American Library Association
APA	American Psychological Association
ASU	Arizona State University
BI	bibliographic instruction
CSE	Council of Science Editors
CSU	California State University
CSUN	California State University Northridge
EMU	Eastern Michigan University
ESL	English as a second language
IATUL	International Association of Technological University Libraries
IL	information literacy
ISP	information search process
LMS	learning management system
MLA	Modern Language Association
MPAA	Motion Picture Association of America
PAIR	Paper Authority Integrity Research
TESOL	teaching English to speakers of other languages
UCSB	University of California Santa Barbara
UNI	University of Northern Iowa
WAC	writing across the curriculum
WID	writing in the disciplines
WPA	Council of Writing Program Administrators

Preface

The purpose of this book is twofold: to provide a discussion about the roles librarians and libraries can play in working to prevent plagiarism, and to offer examples of ways to combat student plagiarism through collaboration with teaching faculty and information literacy instructors. For academic librarians, the rise of concern about plagiarism among faculty and administrators on many college campuses has often led to initiatives and programs that have identified their library as a possible ally. From discussions of whether or not to implement a campus-wide subscription to the plagiarism-detection software Turnitin.com to the creation of information literacy tutorials advising students on how to cite external information correctly in their research – librarians have been working hard to answer campus concerns about plagiarism.

Some may question why librarians and libraries are often seen as natural partners in the fight to educate and/or to enforce policies pertaining to plagiarism. However, after conducting extensive research and reviewing current discussions in many information literacy forums such as listservs and conferences in the past three years, it is evident that a good number of libraries and librarians see a strong connection between educating students about plagiarism and their work to increase student information literacy skills. Still, there are those who would argue that educating students about plagiarism falls out of the spectrum and overall roles and responsibilities of librarianship. Often citing the fact that writing centers and teaching faculty have a greater responsibility to educate students about the dangers of plagiarism, those who discourage librarians from taking an interest fail to see the current connections and historic foundations this role has within librarianship. After all, the full-text databases to which libraries currently subscribe ultimately connect students to the external information that they are in danger of automatically 'cutting and pasting' into their papers. Despite the emerging exportation features that offer formatting in either international citation standards or bibliographic citation management software, many students remain unaware of the advantages of utilizing these tools. If the corporate vendors from which libraries purchase aggregated indexes and other online resources are bothering to try to make the vital connection to proper citation methods via their interfaces, the least librarians and libraries can do is work harder to educate students on how to do this properly through instruction – ensuring that students understand why they must cite and how to do so ethically.

Review of contents

This book is divided into eight chapters. Chapter 1 investigates society's pervasive culture of copying in order to equip readers with an understanding of the scope of the problem. The second chapter explores what the role of the academic librarian is and could be in terms of combating student plagiarism. Chapter 3 examines how students, faculty and universities view plagiarism, while the fourth chapter reveals how information literacy frameworks and curricula can work to promote the ethical use of information by students. The fifth chapter explores the effectiveness of discipline-based approaches to combating student plagiarism. Chapter 6 discusses the role that faculty-librarian collaborations can play in creating a culture of academic integrity, and the seventh chapter gives examples of instructional modules that provide practical approaches to promoting proper citation methods and the ethical usage of information. The final chapter explores how technology itself may or may not be able to aid educators engaged in the fight to combat student plagiarism through the use of plagiarism-detection software services and subscription citation management software packages.

Intended audience

This book with be of particular interest to the following groups.

- Academic librarians involved in teaching and information literacy initiatives.
- Public librarians looking to provide educational programming about the ethical use of information.
- K–12 librarians working to try to teach students why 'cut-and-paste plagiarism' is both unethical and dangerous.
- Faculty members looking for both partners in and solutions to the growing problem of plagiarism.
- University administrators looking to find ways to reduce instances of academic misconduct.
- Directors of faculty development centers interested in finding ideas for programming about plagiarism.

- Researchers investigating the growing problem of plagiarism, its ties to technology and the lack of educational curricula devoted to combating the problem.

Introduction: technology seems to be changing everything

Upon first glancing at the story 'A merit badge that can't be duplicated' in the 21 October 2006 edition of the *Los Angeles Times* (Pierson, 2006), one might initially have thought that the Motion Picture Association of America (MPAA) and the local Boy Scouts were working together on the topic of piracy following the enormous successes of Disney's *Pirates of the Caribbean* films. However, what was really being reported was that officials of both associations were announcing the creation of a 'Respect Copyrights Activity Patch – emblazoned with a large circle "C" copyright sign along with a film reel and musical notes' (ibid.).

Figure I.1   Respect Copyrights activity patch

What is this all about? Why are 52,000 Scouts in the Los Angeles area being targeted to earn an anti-piracy patch by participating in a curriculum produced by the MPAA? According to the article, to earn the badge Scouts must participate in several activities, 'including creating a video public-service announcement and visiting a video sharing website to identify which materials are copyrighted. They may also watch a movie and discuss how people behind the scenes would be harmed if the film were pirated' (ibid.). An entire curriculum has been established to help parents and volunteers engage youngsters in the concept and reality that 'intellectual property is no different than physical property' (Motion Picture Association of America, 2006b).

This might appear to be an unlikely tactic by the MPAA to get people, in this case young boys, to understand copyright laws and the ethical lessons that need to be learned. But in reality the curriculum is much needed both outside and inside classrooms. Warnings against piracy that play at the start of motion picture DVDs and anti-piracy measures implemented by the music recording industry have not successfully deterred enough people from pirating films and sharing illegal copies of movies and music. According to recent reports, MPAA studios lost $6.1 billion to piracy in 2005, with $1.3 billion coming from piracy in the USA and $4.8 billion occurring internationally (Motion Picture Association of America, 2006a).

Regardless of whether or not one is a boy scout, many would agree that more people need to become both educated and respectful about the rules that protect copyright and intellectual property in the age of cut-and-paste creation and peer-to-peer network file sharing. According to a 2005 *Pew Internet Report*, the rationale given by many teenagers who knowingly download files containing copyright-protected video or music is that 'everyone is doing it', and they 'simply switch to new file sharing applications when one becomes popular and copyright holders start "cracking down"' (Lenhart and Madden, 2005). When asked to share their views about opposition to illegally obtained music files or other forms of piracy, many respondents interviewed for the Pew study stated that they felt they received mixed messages as consumers when they are sold CD burners, DVD burners and blank CDs (ibid.).

The recent move by the MPAA to work with the Boy Scouts of America to create an educational curriculum to thwart intellectual property theft signals a paradigm shift that many, both within and outside of educational circles, should replicate. This program's thrust to instruct young people about what constitutes piracy represents an important shift away from over-reliance on reactive and/or punitive responses as the preferred solution to combating piracy. One only hopes that a large portion of the planned curriculum includes information on what constitutes permissible fair use of copyright-protected materials, as well as ethical documentation. As Henry Jenkins (2006: 189) rightly points out, for too long

> Industry groups have tended to address copyright issues primarily through a piracy model, focusing on the threat of file sharing... their official educational materials have been criticized for focusing on copyright protections to the exclusion of any reference to fair use. By implication, fans are seen simply as 'pirates' who steal from the studios and give nothing in return.

Ironically, Jenkins's observation also accurately describes the way that the majority within higher education narrowly handle the problem of plagiarism. The current culture of detection, characterized by infrequently held discussions of punishment and the consequences for acts of plagiarism and academic dishonesty, strongly outweighs proactive efforts to create a curriculum that educates students about the proper ways to incorporate external materials into their writing or projects. While there are many instances of students who intentionally cheat or commit unethical acts which violate academic honor codes, there are larger numbers of students who remain unaware and uneducated about the proper ways to cite materials and conduct research ethically. Moreover, within higher education circles curriculum and/or pedagogical approaches are seldom created to engage students in learning about what constitutes plagiarism and how to avoid it responsibly.

Reflecting on the need for anti-plagiarism and broader information ethics programming to spread into wider circles outside the K–12 age range, I cannot help but remember the events I witnessed at a concert in California. On 17 September 2006 I went to see a live performance by Cyndi Lauper, a famous American pop star. Nothing about this concert tempted me to think about work or my research for this book until Ms Lauper abruptly stopped singing her hit 1984 Billboard number one song *Time After Time*, out of utter disgust and disappointment with an audience member who had decided it was OK to videotape her performance illegally. As best I can recall, Ms Lauper told the audience member taping her: 'Hey, I know that you are going to just load this on to YouTube, so knock it off!'

The tensions between Ms Lauper's attempt to protect her artistic and intellectual property rights and the growing practices of a peer-to-peer publishing culture were palpable in this brief and bizarre moment of the concert. A couple of weeks after the performance, out of sheer curiosity, I logged into YouTube.com (which has since been purchased by Google) to see if Cyndi Lauper's hunch about the audience member's base intentions was correct. Sure enough, almost half the live performance in Agoura Hills, California, had been captured and uploaded to the popular website. The YouTube member who posted the video clips apparently disregarded the site's warnings on uploading videos of live concerts, even if one captured the video oneself. YouTube.com warns users that:

> Even if you took the video yourself, the performer controls the right to use his/her image in a video, the songwriter owns the rights to the song being performed, and sometimes the venue prohibits filming without permission, so this video is likely to infringe somebody else's rights. (YouTube.com, 2007)

Clearly, YouTube's admonition had not stopped those who uploaded portions of video capturing the performance from that night. Moreover, no one had yet intervened to ask to have the materials taken off the website.

How random, and yet likely, that I came face to face with a real-life example which epitomizes how society's beliefs about the protective terms of the ownership of creative material have shifted at a concert. It seems that everywhere one turns nowadays there is a new story about the illegal or unethical usage of text, music, film or art. A review of Richard Posner's *The Little Book of Plagiarism* in the 28 January 2007 *Los Angeles Times* book review section characterizes the current global preoccupation with plagiarism as a 'current craze for searching out, denouncing and punishing authors who appear to have borrowed the work of others and passed it off as their own' (Kirsch, 2007). Whether we are talking about the proliferation of instances of purloined texts that have been cut and pasted into students' plagiarized term papers or the recording of snippets from live performances uploaded to sites like YouTube.com, growing segments of society feel that file sharing and peer-to-peer co-creation overwrite the laws and ethics that outline copyright and attempt to protect intellectual property.

We are facing a mounting crisis. Confusion abounds among many young people about the limits of 'free usage' when it comes to materials found online. Students from primary school to college are interacting with information in different ways than previous generations ever thought possible. The changing information-seeking behavior and information consumption patterns of the emerging millennial generation are forcing many, both within and outside of education circles, to rethink how we should work to teach young people to work ethically with information.

As Lorenzo et al. (2006: 2) note in their paper 'How choice, co-creation, and culture are changing what it means to be net savvy':

> Students who have grown up with the Internet appear to use information technology and online information effortlessly... Constantly connected to information and each other, students don't just consume information. They create and re-create it. With a do-it-yourself, open source approach to material, students often take existing material, add their own touches, and republish it. Bypassing traditional authority channels, self-publishing – in print, image, video, or audio – is common. Access and exchange of information is nearly instantaneous.

So does anyone care about the types of unethical online behavior that many students are engaging in enough to do something proactive about it? Or are too many people willing to stand by until problems arise and have to be addressed? Have we all become too lenient in terms of stopping plagiarism and copyright abuse by continuing to take a predominately reactive stance to thwarting the problem rather than creating proactive educational approaches?

After all, the 'safe harbour' provision of the 1998 Digital Millennium Copyright Act is viewed by many as adequate protection for corporations like Google that own websites and web services like YouTube.com from copyright violations that can be attributed to user postings. As David Drummond, Google's general counsel and senior vice-president of corporate development, noted after Google's purchase of YouTube.com: 'A number of courts have held that under this provision, websites are not liable for copyrighted content posted by users, as long as they promptly remove it when it is pointed out to them' (*Sydney Morning Herald*, 2006). Ironically, corporations and other entities, both individuals and associations, which feel that their intellectual property and ownership of materials are being infringed certainly care enough to threaten to take legal action against those who violate copyright or intellectual property protections.

It seems almost certain that a multitude of lawsuits and media compromises will emerge in the coming years to accommodate the changing landscape. Yet at the same time corporations are also poised to take hold of the money that stands to be made by incorporating the social networking tools of the millennial generation into the already well-established venues of the internet. Lines will continue to be blurred as we find ourselves living in what one scholar,

Henry Jenkins, has coined the 'convergence culture'. Jenkins aptly chooses the term to describe the evolving relationship of three powerful concepts – media convergence, participatory culture and collective intelligence. According to Jenkins (2006: 3):

> Convergence occurs within the brains of individual consumers and through their social interactions with others. Each of us constructs our own personal mythology from bits and fragments of information extracted from the media flow and transformed into resources through which we make sense of our everyday lives.

Describing, for instance, how young Harry Potter fans who created and published their own online fictional Hogwarts tales were accused of stealing the intellectual property of Warner Brothers, Jenkins's work represents an important cultural and media-focused study of how the information explosion is changing the way individuals, especially the young, view intellectual property and how this challenges existing information ethics.

While the examples discussed above are clearly not 'classic' plagiarism violations, the argument needs to be made that students' growing lack of clarity about the concept of intellectual property as a whole leads to acts of plagiarism. Studies have shown that students cannot typically distinguish between what constitutes a copyright or intellectual property violation and what constitutes plagiarism. This common confusion about the two concepts, plagiarism and copyright, does not solely reside in their differences from each other.

While copyright and plagiarism are clearly different areas of concern that have different parameters and rules for prosecuting violations, it is important to mention that academic librarians often lament the blurring of these two separate concepts within the undergraduate and academic population. I believe that student plagiarism should be the first area of concern on which librarians and faculty focus their efforts when confronting the unethical use and/or misuse of information in student work.

As John W. Snapper (1999: 127) wisely pointed out in his article 'On the web, plagiarism matters more than copyright piracy':

> Although commonly confused, the values inherent in copyright policy are different from those inherent in scholarly standards for proper accreditation of ideas. Piracy is the infringement of a copyright, and plagiarism is the failure to give credit. The increasing use of Web-based electronic publication has created new contexts for both piracy and plagiarism... Situations emerge daily for which we have no clear standards either for copyright or for scholarly accreditation.

As Richard Posner explains in *The Little Book of Plagiarism*, the term 'plagiarism' is difficult to define. 'A typical definition is "literary theft." The definition is incomplete because there can be plagiarism of music, pictures, or ideas, as well as of verbal matter' (Posner, 2007: 11). An example of a somewhat broader recent application of this definition of what 'constitutes' plagiarism can be seen in the January 2007 accusations made against Hollywood actor and director Mel Gibson. Juan Catlett, the director of the 1991 film *Return to Aztlan*, accused Mel Gibson of plagiarizing his ideas and scenes in his 2006 film *Apocalypto*. According to a report in *Guardian Unlimited*

(2007), 'Catlett alleges that Gibson asked for a copy of his film while shooting *Apocalypto* and that scenes from *Return to Aztlan* ended up in Gibson's film'. While this latest accusation and subsequent legal investigation into cinematic plagiarism may cynically cause many to remember the witticism of the late Doris Lessing, who stated that 'The only ism Hollywood believes in is plagiarism', the fact remains that creative ideas are increasingly mimicked and copied into both visual and textual texts at a rapid and often highly accepted rate within our society. Many times these incidents are overlooked, or rightly viewed as parodies or homage. However, many questionable media-based examples, from both film and television, are incorrectly dismissed as inter-textual examples, satire or 'compliments'; there are some who believe that the only sensible verdict and definition of these examples is plagiarism or the outright theft of an idea, image, product, etc.

So why should the claims of plagiarism against Mel Gibson for *Apocalypto* signal an opportunity for instruction librarians and other faculty to reach out to students about plagiarism issues? I believe this incident, and others like it, are a chance for instructional librarians to educate students to see how plagiarism accusations and documented intellectual theft cases play out in the 'real world'. Regardless of whether or not real-life cases are 'high-profile' or obscure incidents of plagiarism, they offer students precautionary and disciplinary-based examples that can help in learning how to avoid using information unethically. As Ken Bain (2004: 115) notes in his book *What the Best College Teachers Do*:

> The most effective teachers use class time to help students think about information and ideas the way

scholars in the discipline do… They do not think only in terms of teaching their discipline; they think about teaching *students* to understand, apply, synthesize and evaluate evidence and conclusions.

Real-life examples of how to use or synthesize outside information correctly and incorrectly are critical to students learning how to use and incorporate externally gathered information ethically.

More importantly for the discussions that will take place in this book, students have a very difficult time understanding why they have done something wrong or illegal in terms of their usages of previously created texts, images, sounds or other works. Ken Bain (ibid.: 174) urges all of us involved in teaching students to consider that 'part of being a good teacher is knowing about… these particular students at this particular time and their particular sets of aspirations, confusions, misconceptions and ignorance'.

Students' misunderstandings and lack of education about what actions, within both academic and real-world settings, constitute plagiarism or intellectual property violations present particularly large areas of concern for educators as more and more students are entering college with almost a purely 'internet-only' perspective. As Donald McCabe (2001a), a highly respected authority on academic integrity research in the USA, notes:

> Clearly, plagiarism has gone on forever. However, new electronic technologies raise several difficult points. In particular, students can plagiarize assignments with greater anonymity while using the internet as opposed to getting a paper from someone else or going to the library to get materials to plagiarize. At the moment, my research suggests that the primary issue is an

increase in the amount of plagiarism by students who are already plagiarizing using written sources, and that the increase in the number of new plagiarizers is rather modest. However, as more internet plagiarism occurs, I'm sure this will encourage other students to do the same unless faculty and school address this issue more effectively.

So what role, if any, should librarians take in educating students about these and related issues? This book will focus on this and other important questions. Has technology changed everything in terms of how students view information and their habits in terms of interacting with the materials they access online? Will Turnitin.com help faculty clear up misunderstandings about the institutional rules that define plagiarism on their campuses? Why should academic librarians and faculty consider discipline-based approaches to combating student plagiarism? And what do plagiarism and copyright infringement have to do with information literacy?

The need to educate students about efficient and ethical ways to interact with information continues to grow with each entering freshman class. Within the field of library and information science, and particularly within academic librarianship, the drive to make sure that students retrieve and use information efficiently and ethically has grown into the field of information literacy studies. When the information literacy movement emerged in the early 1990s librarians and other educators were striving to increase student awareness and education surrounding the usage of information in the digital age. The authors of the ACRL *Information Literacy Competency Standards for Higher Education* intended to guide librarians and educators to the best ways to improve students' abilities to 'recognize when information is needed and have the ability to locate, evaluate, and use effectively the needed information' (Association of College and Research Libraries, 2000). The fifth standard of the document calls for students to understand fully the economic, legal and social issues surrounding the use of information, and to access and use information ethically and legally.

Much as the ACRL *Information Literacy Competency Standards* have been adapted into the curricular learning objectives and goals of many libraries and universities, the fifth standard has been the most difficult to implement in terms of creating meaningful educational programming within academic libraries. This book aims to offer librarians and other educators informative ideas about how to educate students better about the dangers of plagiarism and the techniques for ethically and effectively incorporating the information they find through research into their own work.

While some may argue that information literacy is simply a set of skills or attributes to which students need to be exposed during their studies, I tend to side with Johnston and Webber's (2005) contention that a clearly described discipline of information literacy has emerged – a powerful intellectual and pedagogical force for coherence and relevance, and not just a new term for library user education, research skills or generic attributes. Focusing on three elements – information literacy for citizenship, information literacy for economic growth and information literacy for employability – Johnston and Webber correctly maintain that, in terms of preparing citizens for managing and taking action in society, information literacy has much to contribute, and thus it is imperative to support this emergent discipline (ibid.). While aspects of information literacy educational programming clearly have a personal lifelong learning educational aspect (such as improving an individual's searching capabilities), the ethical use of information is an education goal that all of higher education and society at large should embrace in light of the current problems we face.

Certainly it is often true that a researcher starts to see traces of his or her research in all aspects of daily life due to his/her dedication to a project. In my case, my job as a reference and instruction librarian offers many chances to glimpse into the patterns of students' usages of information. While I may have more opportunities than most people to provide educational guidance to those currently befuddled by the infinite choices that can be made in terms of the acquisition, retrieval, manipulation and dissemination of information, I am still often amazed at how profoundly the landscape and the concepts of ownership, attribution, intellectual property and academic honesty have changed in the past decade. I make a conscious effort to engage students continually about the issues surrounding the ethical uses of information. Interestingly, in doing this I have found that students are receptive and interested to receive guidance, counselling and further information about such things as proper citation, paraphrasing and discipline-based standards in the area of documenting research.

In a November 2006 article, Matthew K. Dames labeled plagiarism the 'new piracy', since it has 'become the hot, new *crime du jour* – an act that suggests immorality and often scandal at once'. However, as those who have studied plagiarism know, it is hardly a new act. The concept of plagiarism has a very long history, and according to the *Oxford English Dictionary* the word itself comes from a Latin word 'plagiary', whose etymology is defined as containing the classical Latin meaning of *plagirius* as a person who abducts the child or slave of another, a kidnapper, seducer and also a literary thief. For the purposes of this book plagiarism will be defined as the act of using someone else's ideas or words without crediting the source in a manner that is accepted by the field or discipline within which the plagiarist is studying or working. The focus of this book is largely on how academic librarians can work to combat the culture of plagiarism that currently exists among students. In addition, it will touch upon how intellectual property theft looms as a larger and allied concern in terms of student understanding of the issues that surround the ethical usage of information.

Today, acts of plagiarism are often conflated with other intellectual property crimes, such as copyright theft and/or infringements. But currently plagiarism tends to ruin and/or taint an individual's reputation much more than a copyright violation does within and outside of academe.

> Plagiarism accusations can dog and derail professional careers, even of those who have made legitimate or honest errors. The best way to stay out of plagiarism's bright, unflattering spotlight is to identify citation customs (these will differ according to industry), learn those customs and citation standards, and where possible seek training or assistance in mastering and applying these standards. (Dames, 2006)

If you can acknowledge the concept that information literacy, and in particular a student's understanding of the best ways to use information ethically, is a critical thought process needed in the age of information and search, I believe that you will embrace many of the ideas and strategies discussed in this book. It aims to show how academic librarians and all educators can help combat student plagiarism through proactive efforts and practical approaches geared to effecting change in students' uses of information and ideas that were not originally their own.

1

Society's pervasive culture of copying

> People who would never dream of stealing a necklace or a CD will cut-and-paste a passage from the net into their paper without a moment's hesitation and in complete ignorance of any prohibitions against such behavior. In a world of shareware, free expression, and easy access to Internet information, no one thinks of acknowledging the original source of words or ideas. Information is all one big floating, evanescent, amorphous mass. (Roth, 1999)

On 23 April 2006 it was reported in Harvard University's student newspaper, *The Harvard Crimson*, that one of its most celebrated undergraduates, Kaavya Viswanathan, had been accused of rampant acts of plagiarism in her recently released book *How Opal Mehta Got Kissed, Got Wild, and Got A Life: A Novel*. Ms Viswanathan's fall from grace was doggedly covered by the media, which seemed mesmerized by yet another story of an overachieving young author falling to accusations of plagiarism. The identified plagiarized text in the novel led Viswanathan's publisher, Little, Brown and Company, to pull remaining copies of the newly released novel from bookstores. The publisher released a statement saying: 'Little, Brown and Company will not be publishing a revised edition of *How Opal Mehta Got Kissed, Got Wild, and Got a Life* by Kaavya Viswanathan, nor will we publish the second book under contract' (Italie, 2006). Not only was Viswanthan's lucrative pre-publication book deal for $500,000 in jeopardy; Hollywood also moved into immediate damage-control mode over the crestfallen young author's predicament. Within a week of the story breaking in *The Harvard Crimson*, DreamWorks reportedly backed out of its pending film agreement with Viswanathan.

Since Ms Viswanathan's fall, many have voiced differing views on the levels of her guilt or innocence. The young author herself never admitted that she intentionally plagiarized numerous passages from Megan McCafferty's *Sloppy Firsts* and *Second Helpings* and other published works. In a statement released by Little, Brown and Company, Viswanathan did state that:

> When I was in high school, I read and loved two wonderful novels by Megan McCafferty, *Sloppy Firsts* and *Second Helpings*, which spoke to me in a way few other books did. Recently, I was very surprised and upset to learn that there are similarities between some passages in my novel... and passages in these books. While the central stories of my book and her's are completely different, I wasn't aware of how much I may have internalized Ms. McCafferty's words. I am a huge fan of her work and can honestly say that any phrasing similarities between her works and mine were completely unintentional and unconscious. My publisher and I plan to revise my novel for future printings to eliminate any inappropriate similarities. I

sincerely apologize to Megan McCafferty and to any who feel they have been misled by these unintentional errors on my part. (Mehegan, 2006)

After the release of Ms Viswanathan's statement regarding the reports of alleged plagiarism in her novel, McCafferty's publisher Random House issued the following statement:

> We find both the responses of Little Brown and their author Kaayva Viswanathan deeply troubling and disingenuous. Ms. Viswanathan's claim that similarities in her phrasing were 'unconscious' or 'unintentional' is suspect. We have documented more than forty passages from Kaavya Viswanathan's recent publication '*How Opal Mehta Got Kissed, Got Wild, and Got a Life*' that contain identical language and/or common scene or dialogue structure from Megan McCafferty's first two books, '*Sloppy Firsts*' and '*Second Helpings*.' This extensive taking from Ms. McCafferty's books is nothing less than an act of literary identity theft. Based on the scope and character of the similarities, it is inconceivable that this was a display of youthful innocence or an unconscious or unintentional act. (Random House, 2006)

What Viswanathan, Little, Brown and others failed to expose was the role of the book-packaging company involved in the development of *How Opal Mehta Got Kissed, Got Wild, and Got a Life*. According to John Barlow (2006): 'Book packaging is not a new phenomenon. It involves getting a book concept together, thus saving the publisher the trouble of finding writers, illustrators, editors, etc. Then a finished concept is sold to a publisher as a *fait accompli.*' The fact that Viswanathan's novel was produced by a book-packaging company, Alloy Entertainment, deserves serious attention. According to Anne Schleicher (2006): 'Book packaging companies share the copyright with authors as well as any advances or royalties the author might receive.' Schleicher also interviewed Karen Holt, deputy editor of *Publisher's Weekly*, who revealed where part of the blame may lie in terms of texts not being checked for plagiarism or factual accuracy. Holt stated, 'In a sense, in a lot of cases it's [book packaging] a form of outsourcing for the publisher, where a lot of the editorial functions that you would assume that a publisher is doing actually the book packager is doing' (ibid.).

How did Viswanathan come to work with a book packager? After all, it seems a bit strange that a 17-year-old author was approached in high school to follow through on a book idea. With a story that could have easily been chronicled in *The Overachievers: The Secret Lives of Driven Kids* (Robbins, 2006), it is not too surprising to learn that Kaavya Viswanathan's initial ideas and work on the novel *How Opal Mehta Got Kissed, Got Wild, and Got a Life* were reportedly discovered during her introduction to Katherine Cohen of IvyWise, a college consulting company.

Like many other highly successful high school applicants and their parents who yearn to get into the college or university of their dreams, Kaavya Viswanathan and her family sought out the help of IvyWise. Cohen, according to Mark Patinkin (2006):

> is one of the most successful college consultants out there. *The New York Times* says she charges $33,000 for two years of consulting. Some parents hire consultants like her for all four high school years for over $40,000... The agency does far more than help

kids with applications. It structures their whole lives – for years – to enhance their chances. IvyWise pushes kids toward language-immersion summers abroad, uses connections to get them high-powered internships, and advises at least 100 hours a year of volunteering.

According to Patinkin, when Katherine Cohen of IvyWise learned that her client Viswanathan was a budding writer, she sent the few chapters that Kaavya had completed to her literary agent. The concept for Kaavya's book was then further developed by Alloy Entertainment. Patinkin (ibid.) notes that 'Even Alloy's president [Leslie Morgenstein] has been quoted as saying that his firm only "helped Kaavya conceptualize and plot the book".' Alloy Entertainment, Little, Brown and IvyWise certainly did not create the instances of plagiarism that can be found in *How Opal Mehta Got Kissed, Got Wild, and Got a Life*, as Ms Viswanathan authored the book. However, it is important to mention that these three entities should have taken some responsibility in checking the authenticity of the work. After all, it is not as if Viswanathan's book was the first novel of 2006 to have come under scrutiny for literary crimes. In January 2006 James Frey's 'memoir', *A Million Little Pieces*, an Oprah Winfrey Book Club selection, was exposed for factual misrepresentation and outright deception. In that same year publishers and their scrutiny in terms of editorial responsibilities for textual accuracy were also called into question in light of the accusations of plagiarism leveled against Dan Brown, the author of the worldwide bestseller *The Da Vinci Code*.

Ultimately the author of any fictional or non-fictional text bears the responsibility for ensuring the accuracy and authenticity of the work. However, in a day and age where the reproduction and/or outright copying of creative ideas is a huge industry, we should also be questioning where society's responsibility lies in raising awareness about the problem of plagiarism and intellectual theft. If book packagers like Alloy Entertainment and 17th Street are marketing their services to newly minted Generation Y or even younger authors, it is important for educators and parents to make sure that a greater understanding about the ethics and practices needed to write or conduct research accurately is promulgated and introduced to young writers and researchers.

In actuality, Viswanathan's involvement with Alloy Entertainment exposes another underlying theme in this story, revealing the pressures that many young authors and students may find themselves operating under in terms of achieving academic or literary success. It may also shed light on the common pressures that lead growing numbers of authors and students to participate in a culture of copying and cheating. As David Callahan (2004) notes in his book *The Cheating Culture: Why More Americans Are Doing Wrong to Get Ahead*, the recent increase in high-profile incidents of plagiarism, cheating and other forms of unethical behavior in the area of publishing and the dissemination of information is emblematic of a serious trend. Peer pressure and increasing parental expectations for students to succeed at levels of perfection add pressure to today's young people. Callahan (ibid.: 13) writes:

> These stories are not isolated instances. They are part of a pattern of widespread cheating throughout U.S. society. By its nature cheating is intended to go undetected, and trends in unethical behavior are hard to document. Still, available evidence strongly suggests that Americans are not only cheating more in many

areas but are also feeling less guilty about it. When 'everybody does it,' or imagines that everybody does it, a cheating culture has emerged.

The growth of a culture of copying and cheating is occurring in concert with a decrease in individuals' sense of adherence to a culture of academic integrity. As reported on a 2004 episode of the popular American television news show *Primetime Live*:

> According to one survey, The Josephson Institute of Ethics Report Card (2002), often cited by educators themselves, of 12,000 high school students, 74 percent, almost three-quarters, admitted cheating on an examination at least once in the past year. This might make you wonder, what's going on at my child's school? Or at schools I once attended? And you wonder, what does all that cheating say about all of us? (ABC News, 2004)

The show's anchor, Charles Gibson, interviewed a number of US high school students for this episode, which aired on 29 April. Gibson's interviews revealed that a surprising number of those questioned had created their own system of moral reasoning that allowed them to feel comfortable about cheating. One of the college students interviewed stated the rationale for cheating in the following manner: 'There's other people getting better grades than me and they're cheating. Why am I not going to cheat? It's kind of almost stupid if you don't. I don't feel smart enough compared to people who cheat next to me, you know' (ibid.).

Questions about plagiarism, one of the types of cheating exposed as a growing problem in this particular broadcast, were also posed to the students Gibson interviewed. When asked about why they felt OK about plagiarizing, one high school student commented, 'Not on everything. I think the general student body believes that, yeah, on some things, if you have to. Or if you have a whole lot of assignments due on the same date or very close to each other' (ibid.).

Data compiled by Donald McCabe, director of the Center for Academic Integrity, show that:

> Internet plagiarism is a growing concern on all campuses as students struggle to understand what constitutes acceptable use of the Internet. In the absence of clear direction from faculty, most students have concluded that 'cut & paste' plagiarism – using a sentence or two (or more) from different sources on the Internet and weaving this information together into a paper without appropriate citation – is not a serious issue. While 10% of students admitted to engaging in such behavior in 1999, almost 40% admit to doing so in the Assessment Project surveys. A majority of students (77%) believe such cheating is not a very serious issue. (Center for Academic Integrity, 2005)

A 1999 *US & News World Report* survey established that '90 percent of students believe that cheaters are either never caught or have not been appropriately disciplined' (Kleiner and Lord, 1999). This undoubtedly leads many students to believe that plagiarism and other acts of academic dishonesty are probably not a big deal, and therefore engaging in acts of cheating like plagiarism is not likely to be thought about twice without preventive educational programming.

Today's society and the young people coming of age in it are truly facing a complex world where it is becoming increasingly difficult to discern where information originated and/or its authenticity. Critical thinking skills and the decision-making that goes into research and other creative processes are often muddled by the overabundance of external information that one can bring into the synthesis of a product. Computer software, blogs, Facebook, YouTube and the growth of community publishing through other vehicles like fan postings for reality TV shows, social networking sites and various popular forms of media continue to change the way that people think about the steps needed to publish their ideas and/or to synthesize and sometimes 'borrow' the ideas of others.

The work of Henry Jenkins, the author of *Convergence Culture: Where Old and New Media Collide*, firmly establishes how emerging generations are finding themselves often trapped in situations where the 'story of American arts in the twenty-first century might be told in terms of the public reemergence of grassroots creativity as everyday people take advantage of new technologies that enable them to archive, annotate, appropriate, and recirculate media content' (Jenkins, 2006: 136). Jenkins eloquently describes our 'convergence culture' by discussing how our emerging practices in light of the technological revolution allow us both to consume and to create media simultaneously at accelerated speeds and levels. An example of this can be seen in the growth of plagiarism in blogging. In a 10 May 2006 posting on his blog *Plagiarism Today*, Jonathan Bailey describes the bloggers who steal blocks of text from other bloggers, a process known as 'scrapping', as 'a new breed of content users that walk a gray area between that which is clearly fair use and what is obviously content theft. Their blogs are marked with large swaths of block quotes and heavy content reuse, but also proper attribution and at least some original content' (Bailey, 2006).

The plagiarism that is taking place is not only on hobbyist blogs. Scandals have arisen and legal actions have been taken concerning professional blogs and bloggers that have fallen under plagiarism allegations. Take the case of Ben Domenech, a *Washington Post* blogger and journalist who was forced to resign after facing accusations of copying articles from other blogs and publications (Bosman, 2006a). As Del Jones reported in an August 2006 article:

> In some quarters, plagiarism remains a serious offense. But where it involves the Internet, an acceptance of plagiarism is taking hold, and when confronted, offenders often shrug it off as hardly newsworthy. Pew Research two weeks ago said it found that of the 12 million adults who blog, 44% say they have taken songs, text or images and 'remixed' them into their own artistic creation.

This is not to say that blogging inherently leads to plagiarism, but it is important to note that some internet software spam programs are automatically programmed to 'scrap' blog content. Jones (ibid.) notes that 'software used by spammers automatically and intentionally grab original content to post on blogs and Internet sites', causing online authors to become the 'byproduct victims of an attempt to draw traffic to the content so that readers will click on deceiving links that take them to advertising'.

High-profile and notable cases of blog text being misattributed or unethically posted signal the larger attribution problems that can emerge in a social networking web environment where bloggers can quickly publish accurate or inaccurate quotes, thereby possibly causing considerable damage. A recent example that epitomizes this situation can be seen in the 2006 squabble between political commentator Arianna Huffington and Hollywood actor George Clooney. Clooney contended that Huffington, who has her own blog, the *Huffington Post*, asked him to write a post for her blog. Huffington's camp contended that Clooney said that he 'didn't know how a blog worked'. As Tom Zeller Jr (2006) reported:

> The basic facts are not in dispute. Ms. Huffington wanted Mr. Clooney – an outspoken critic of the war and American foreign policy – blogging on her site, but the actor, she said, wasn't familiar with the form. So she culled some published Clooneyisms – essentially answers to questions he'd been asked in previous interviews – fashioned them into an essaylike blog entry, and added a few flourishes of her own, including the punchy 'I am a liberal. Fire away.' bit.

Clooney's representatives and later George Clooney himself, pointed out that the blog entry was not written by Clooney. '"These are not my writings – they are answers to questions and there is a huge difference," Mr. Clooney said.' (Ibid.)

Misattribution, whether intentional or accidental, is an area of confusion that often plagues students regardless of whether they are journalists or writing a term paper. The problem usually stems from students not understanding how to quote, paraphrase or cite correctly. Clearly, the Huffington/Clooney battle is largely a by-product of the inconsistent practices and standards of writers and publishing in the blogosphere. But the rate at which these mistakes can be copied and transmitted to misinform the public in the online world should send alarm waves out to educators that there are increasingly important reasons, outside of traditional publication structures, which merit an increase in attention to educating students about ethical attribution and citation. Media platforms are changing, and the consumers of information are increasingly becoming the creators of that information as well.

Consumers of all ages now have seemingly ubiquitous access to and a greater influence over the future directions of media due to the growth of participatory cultural practices. The trends that Jenkins (2006) identifies in *Convergence Culture: Where Old and New Media Collide* reveal the blurring of the roles between creative producers or authors and their audience. The lines between the creator of a form of intellectual property and the consumers have been carelessly smudged by society's increased access to and need to gather products and information instantaneously. This problem is further exacerbated by the information consumer's ability readily to alter and then repackage online content on demand. This means that the days of seeking attribution and documenting sources, as we know it, will be numbered and/or at least challenged, unless those of us within the circles of education re-emphasize the importance of these practices to students in terms of real-world realities and disciplinary and professional practices.

In an effort to study whether or not things have become worse in terms of student cheating, I thought it might be interesting to investigate how my undergraduate alma mater, the University of California Santa Barbara (UCSB), is faring in terms of student plagiarism and cheating. A fairly recent interview conducted by the UCSB student newspaper, *The Daily Nexus*, contained a commonplace and yet accurate observation of why many believe that we have become a culture of copying since the late 1990s. As Lauren Young reported, the number of students found guilty of academic misconduct acts like plagiarism during the

2003–2004 academic year grew, despite the UCSB's efforts to end plagiarism. According to Young (2004):

> In 2002–03 the University handled 27 cases of academic misconduct, including 14 cases of Internet plagiarism, 10 cases of non-Internet plagiarism and three cases of cheating during exams. There were 19 students found guilty of academic misconduct during the Spring and Summer of 2003, of which one was expelled, 16 were suspended and two were put on academic probation.

While these numbers may seem small for a campus population that has close to 20,000 undergraduates, the larger concern is how many cases of plagiarism are going undetected or unreported. As evidenced by reporting in the UCSB *Daily Nexus* student newspaper, as early as 2001 the campus was clearly concerned about internet plagiarism. By 2004, when asked about the culture of copy at the UCSB, the campus conduct educator Brandon Brod quipped, 'These days students don't plagiarize big books, now students just go to Google and type in their topic.' (Ibid.)

Ironically, according to reports the UCSB opted out of a subscription to the plagiarism-detection software Turnitin.com in November 2001 despite positive faculty reactions to the product during the campus's trial subscription period. The decision not to contract with Turnitin.com was largely due to budgetary constraints. Another *Daily Nexus* article, written by Traci Bank (2001), explains how many felt that the threat of the trial subscription to Turnitin.com was perhaps enough to thwart instances of student plagiarism in 2001: 'Last year, approximately 800 students in an introductory art history course were told that the professor would be using

Turnitin.com. None were caught plagiarizing.' Successes like these, and faculty members' individual subscriptions to the service, led the campus to encourage the development of a home-grown system known as PAIRwise (Paper Authority Integrity Research). According to the Center for Information Technology and Society (2007), which hosts the service at the UCSB, the process of using PAIRwise to catch plagiarized texts works as follows.

> Students submit written assignments to a website. PAIRwise then analyzes those assignments and produces a report that identifies instances of likely plagiarism by indicating the percentage of each assignment that shares identical wording with other sources. This information is presented graphically for instructors to use in making their own judgments about whether students have followed instructions for citations, collaboration, and academic integrity.

It was also reported in the *Santa Barbara News Press* that UCSB political science Professor John Woolsey believes that students 'haven't absorbed what most of us consider academic morality. So they take and use without citing' (Green, 2005). Indeed, as reporter Morgan Green (ibid.) notes:

> patterns at UCSB reflect those around the nation... The experts say many of today's college students don't understand that a cyber-source must be attributed with quotation marks or footnotes just as if it were an old-fashioned encyclopedia. Students have become accustomed to downloading music and movies and sharing with friends, even though such items are usually for sale.

In addition to exploring commercial software and detection services like Turnitin.com or creating home-grown systems like PAIRwise, at universities around the country libraries and campus administrators are also now investigating the practicality of bibliographic management software packages, like RefWorks and EndNote, which help both students and faculty in the documentation process as they write their papers. These trends and citation management software products will be discussed further in Chapter 8 of this book.

So why should librarians and other educators working at colleges and universities around the globe care about the rampant increase in cheating and the culture of copying? Have things become considerably worse in the past ten to 20 years? Or are we merely experiencing another punctuated equilibrium within human history, brought about by technological innovations that challenge traditional understandings of the proper and ethical dissemination of reported or published information? Will the rise in blogging and wikis and the emergence of other highly dynamic collaborative community publication structures further fragment students' conceptions of needing to cite sources, and moreover how and when citation needs to occur within different disciplines?

I believe that the problem of plagiarism has become worse over the last decade. Much of this has been caused by a blurring of the lines in terms of where students perceive they need to go to get their information from physically. Gone are the days of having to head into a reference room at the university library or a local public branch to look up the literature that exists on a term-paper topic in a single source like the *Reader's Guide to Periodical Literature* in print. This is not to say that the emergence of online full-text indexing and abstract article databases and services is a bad thing. But the choices and gradations in terms of the types of publications available are overwhelming for typical undergraduates to deal with in their quest to retrieve a couple of sources for their term papers. After a student gathers the information that s/he perceives is needed to complete his/her paper or research project, it seems that documenting the research resources remains a low priority.

Students' lack of awareness of or enthusiasm for creating proper in-text citations and bibliographies may indeed be nothing new within the halls of higher education or high school. But the new problem is that it is becoming increasingly easier for students to commit 'cut-and-paste' plagiarism, both unwittingly and knowingly. The challenge will be for librarians and faculty working on campuses to confront the growing culture of copying by offering meaningful and efficient resources and services that promote the standards of existing scholarly documentation processes to help students avoid plagiarism or the unethical usage of information in their work.

So is it accurate to say that we live in a 'culture of copying'? Yes, I believe it is entirely accurate and responsible to say that we do. Reports of increased instances of plagiarism and breaches of intellectual property rights reveal a substantial change in information consumers' ethics, both within and outside academia, brought on by the technological capabilities that now abound due to the computer revolution. Some may question whether emerging generations of students value intellectual property less than their predecessors. Or have human beings always gravitated towards borrowing from previous examples of knowledge and creation? These are certainly serious questions to ponder. But within the framework of higher education these questions can no longer be allowed to linger. There are too many recent discoveries of blatant plagiarism within academe and everyday life to continue to ignore the growing and dangerous symptoms of a culture of copying any longer. Action must be taken. More importantly, past notions of how to combat plagiarism, cheating and other academic integrity infractions must be re-examined.

It is far too easy to take the position that plagiarism is just something that has always happened, and therefore we should not get into a state of frenzy over every new high-profile case that is brought to our attention through media channels. After the Viswanathan scandal emerged, many high-profile pundits and academics suggested that this example was not worthy of the attention it was garnering, as it was merely a case of plagiarized teen 'chick lit'. Harvard University allowed Kaavya Viswanathan to remain a student, since her acts of plagiarism occurred outside the classroom or coursework. However, according to the *Harvard Magazine* (2006), one way that the university reportedly responded to Ms Viswanathan's fall from grace was removing her from a direct mentoring role in the upcoming freshman orientation program.

Understandably the university faced pressure to take this action from alumni and others within its community. However, it is unfortunate that the one voice which entering Harvard freshmen perhaps needed to hear from in terms of learning the consequences of plagiarism was deemed to be unacceptable and dangerous in a one-on-one peer-mentoring basis. Granted, one cannot assume that Ms Viswanathan would have been willing to participate in a program on plagiarism in order to draw attention to the problem for the purposes of community service. One only hopes that the real-life plagiarism accusations that plagued her and others are used as case studies to illuminate the importance of learning how to use information ethically. Sadly, it seems that it is still usually more acceptable to sweep the high-profile accusations of plagiarism under the rugs of university halls rather than building upon the valuable lessons that students can learn from real-life mistakes.

2

The role of the academic librarian in combating student plagiarism

> Let's face it, there are very few students who really take the time to learn the style guides… What we want to encourage is that [students] do cite appropriately. (Fran Nowakowski, coordinator of information literacy efforts at Dalhousie's Killam Library, quoted in Crawley, 2006)
>
> Our motto is, 'write the paper, not the footnotes'. (Michael Hu, creator of EazyCite Software, quoted in Crawley, 2006)

Librarians around the globe are seeing an increased interest in the problem of student plagiarism from both faculty and administrators and individuals working outside of higher education. However, despite the increased awareness, indecision remains over how to handle the plagiarism problem within the existing roles and responsibilities of librarianship. Should librarians be involved in developing curricular and instructional solutions to combat student plagiarism? Is it appropriate for librarians to teach techniques to students and faculty on ways to avoid plagiarism within instructional sessions? Should libraries offer online self-paced tutorials on citation documentation styles? Or rather, is it more the role of writing instructors, discipline faculty or tutoring centers to work with students on learning how to cite and integrate external information sources ethically into their papers and research? The question of who should be involved in the shared responsibility of teaching students about proper citation and the dangers of plagiarism continues to go unanswered and be debated among both librarians and others within and outside the field of education.

This chapter reviews the literature within library and information science and education, examining how librarians' inability or unwillingness to answer these questions decisively has been going on for decades. It discusses how academic librarians' struggles to gather support cohesively for tackling student plagiarism through library instruction or other efforts mirror the obstacles commonly faced by 'writing across the curriculum' instructors and programs looking for curricular solutions to help improve student writing and research habits. Through a review of the literature, with a particular focus on higher education populations, the chapter will show that the library has often been seen by faculty as a key or tangential ally in detecting student plagiarism and introducing undergraduate students to research methods. In addition, it will discuss both librarians' and faculty members' views on the role that librarians should and could play in combating student plagiarism in the internet age. By debating the various roles that academic librarians and libraries could and/or currently do take in helping to prevent student plagiarism, which have not been thoroughly defined or agreed upon before within the profession, this chapter will set the stage for subsequent chapters which offer examples of implementation solutions and ways to discuss these issues

further with colleagues, faculty, administrators and most
importantly students.

Whose role is it anyway? Teaching students about attribution and citation

To find evidence supporting the notion that librarians
remain indecisive about how to handle plagiarism within
the existing roles and expanding teaching responsibilities of
librarianship, one can look at the logs of listserv discussions
dedicated to the topic. For instance, in November 2006
academic librarians, responding to a general listserv query
about the possible roles and techniques that librarians can
employ in teaching citation style formats, ended up debating
the merits of assisting students in learning how to cite
information using styles like the Modern Language
Association (MLA) or the American Psychological
Association (APA) citation formats (ILI Discussion Listserv,
2006). While many of the posted comments touched upon
the instructional techniques and methods that librarians
currently employ to cover the topic effectively, it was
evident that some respondents were not convinced that
teaching citation styles is an endeavor which academic
librarians should undertake.

One respondent, William Badke (2006), an academic
librarian who frequently contributes to discussions and
publications on information literacy, wrote: 'There is much
more to teach that actually *is* information literacy, so that
being asked to teach style is akin to being asked to teach
academic writing – good topics, wrong venue.' Badke also
later sent a link to an article entitled 'Citation sensation'

(Crawley, 2006), which focuses on the growing trend of having students utilize bibliographic management citation software, such as a program called EazyPaper, in order to free them up to concentrate their efforts on 'writing the paper'. The article suggests that students will get what they need in terms of learning how to cite properly from software products like EazyPaper.

Indeed, many academic libraries and their campuses are moving in the direction of purchasing and/or promoting products like EazyPaper or 'software such as ProCite, EndNote, and Reference Manager (all owned by Thomson ResearchSoft) and the privately held web-based applications like RefWorks that integrate with Microsoft Word to export saved references into papers and to format footnotes and reference lists automatically' (ibid.: 1). However, this software does not adequately help students completely understand how, when and why they need to cite information in the first place. Librarians and faculty will still need to intercede and teach students how to use these products. Time in the classroom will also need to focus on emphasizing the critical thinking aspects involved in deciding when and how to cite information. While these products offer a step forward in curriculum design possibilities, they are likely not self-teaching tools for all students. Librarians and instructors will still need to help many students distinguish what type of information they are working with and how to cite properly.

The move by many libraries and campuses to acquire bibliographic management software that helps researchers organize and/or produce proper citations and references does not signal that discussions of ethical citation behavior and plagiarism should recede or disappear from library and classroom instructional curricula. The software and technology that make electronic bibliographic management possible should actually increase the notion that the job of teaching students how and when to cite properly is part of the roles and responsibilities of librarians and other campus faculty and educators. Many may question why librarians should be involved. I believe the appropriate response to this query is: why not? After all, many bibliographic management software products are designed to connect to full-text library databases and export selected citations via e-mail. It is likely that the absence of proactive librarian involvement in this area of information literacy skills development will allow many students to fall into sloppy hallmark habits of plagiarism by possibly mismanaging or accepting citation results gleaned from library electronic information resources that may not be correct.

Therefore, it seems both premature and foolhardy to hand over fully the required skill of citing information in a preferred style format to software programs that 'handle' the job for students. That would be a bit like having students only use calculators to solve mathematical formulas without their having a basic understanding of mathematical principles. With the vast amount of information and types of information resources readily available today, citing information requires a bit more critical thinking at a certain level than just plugging data into form fields to generate citations. At my own institution, California State University Northridge, librarians urge students to review electronically generated pre-formatted citations (MLA, APA, etc.) carefully. We are well aware that students far too often trustingly export pre-formatted citations from our full-text article databases immediately, placing them 'as is' into their required bibliographies without reviewing for errors. The tendency of students is to accept what the computerized database generates as a complete and correctly formatted citation, in MLA or APA styles. The common assumption is that the database is generating a perfect citation for their paper, sight unseen.

Whether or not one is in favor of promoting subscription bibliographic management software packages and/or the citation export functions that exist in library databases, the November 2006 ILI listserv responses about teaching citation style reveal that librarians are still not in agreement about what role, if any, they should play in educating students to avoid plagiarism by citing information correctly and ethically. There is clearly a hesitance by some librarians to take library instruction and the curricular integration of information literacy student learning outcomes past the traditional comfort zone of refining information retrieval and locating resources. However, clearly what are needed are deeper curricular plans that provide students with practice in making connections from information retrieval into the knowledge-creation phase involved in writing and research. Ironically, these unresolved debates are nothing new to the profession of academic librarianship, and they mirror struggles that occur in other disciplines.

While many librarians are anxious to hear about proven ways to integrate anti-plagiarism instruction into information literacy programming, some may feel that they would be too hard pressed to find the time in a typical 50-minute instructional session to review painstakingly the intricacies of citation style rules included in such formats as APA, MLA or Chicago. Others may agree with those who think that teaching citation styles, standards and information ethics does not fall into information literacy instruction. However, there are clear linkages between citation styles and information literacy visible in both well-established national information literacy student learning outcomes and research. These linkages will be discussed in a later chapter. Understanding and evaluating the information that they choose to incorporate into their own knowledge base or term paper require students' understanding and repeated utilization of citation methods. Moreover, without the ability to cite information correctly students are arguably more apt to commit acts of plagiarism, and that constitutes a lack of information literacy.

Academic libraries and student writing

Before delving into a discussion of how librarians view their role in working to combat student plagiarism, it is important to examine the relationship that academic librarianship and in particular library instructional programming has traditionally held in relation to student academic writing and research. Academic libraries have long supported the development of student research. Librarians have also assisted colleagues working to develop student research projects that complement their writing across the curriculum (WAC) programs. Increasingly, within the recent literature of academic librarianship it is also clear that a growing number of researchers and practitioners agree with the sentiment expressed by Thomas G. Kirk Jr (1995: ix–x):

> The examination of the teaching of writing, particularly WAC (writing across the curriculum) programs, helps librarians understand more clearly the nature of changes in bibliographic instruction… that WAC and BI (bibliographic instruction) are marginal to most academic programs and are isolated from each other… because the revolution in undergraduate

education has not completed the process of synthesizing subject content and process content into an integrated whole.

Information literacy instructional programming efforts are very akin to those of writing composition programs, and this similarity is vital to understanding why anti-plagiarism instruction remains on the fringe of instructional curricula within both of these emerging fields and in academia as a whole.

What are the similarities between writing composition and library instruction programs? There are many; and it is interesting to note that both fields have experienced the emergence of two powerful subfield concentrations since the late 1980s, namely the 'writing across the curriculum' movement and the growth of information literacy. As Barbara Fister (1992: 156) noted in her paper 'Common ground: the composition/bibliographic instruction connection':

> There are obvious connections between the process approach to writing and the librarians' approach of teaching search strategies. When the search behavior of library users or the affective side of research (Carol Kuhlthau and Contance Mellon) are studied librarians [are] exploring the same territory as students of composition.

Fister systematically outlines how the writing and research processes are linked, and this is important for understanding and developing ways to create anti-plagiarism strategies in instructional settings. In her map of the field of composition (Figure 2.1), Fister shows the similarities and important areas of concern that both

Figure 2.1   Map of the field of composition

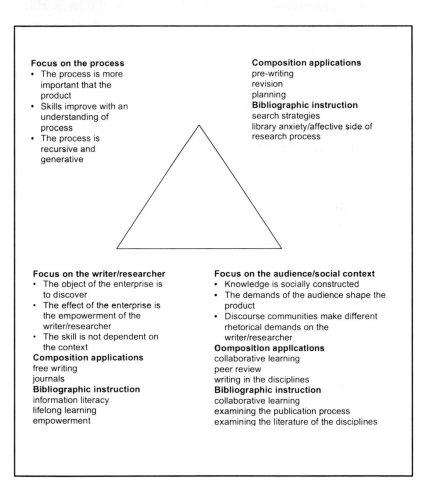

Focus on the process
• The process is more important that the product
• Skills improve with an understanding of process
• The process is recursive and generative

Composition applications
pre-writing
revision
planning
Bibliographic instruction
search strategies
library anxiety/affective side of research process

Focus on the writer/researcher
• The object of the enterprise is to discover
• The effect of the enterprise is the empowerment of the writer/researcher
• The skill is not dependent on the context
Composition applications
free writing
journals
Bibliographic instruction
information literacy
lifelong learning
empowerment

Focus on the audience/social context
• Knowledge is socially constructed
• The demands of the audience shape the product
• Discourse communities make different rhetorical demands on the writer/researcher
Oomposition applIcatIons
collaborative learning
peer review
writing in the disciplines
Bibliographic instruction
collaborative learning
examining the publication process
examining the literature of the disciplines

Source: Fister (1992: 155)

writing instructors and librarians typically have students focus on in class.

In relation to the topic of plagiarism and the focus of librarians on the research and writing process, it seems clear that the similarity which should become of greater focus takes place in the 'audience/social context' that Fister identifies. Building on the research of writing instructors, who emphasize the importance of helping students understand the standards of the discipline within which they are writing, librarians should also begin to see that an emphasis on having students examine how knowledge is socially constructed within the discipline they are studying matters in terms of preventing plagiarism. Once educators accept the need to develop a role in combating student plagiarism, it is clear there are steps that can be taken to help prevent undocumented research writing.

Writing across the curriculum programs and the faculty and staff dedicated to their success represent ideal partners for librarians working to promote students properly documenting external sources. For the purposes of definition:

> Writing Across the Curriculum (also known as WAC) generally refers to an educational initiative which promotes the idea that students who write in every course will not only become better writers, but will also learn course content more effectively. Writing Across the Curriculum is a departure from the traditional teacher-centered, prescriptive approach to teaching writing. (Galvin, 2006: 27)

Like information literacy, the thinking behind WAC pedagogies 'starts from a different view of learning'. Writing is seen as more than a communication skill. It is treated as 'both a process of doing critical thinking and a product communicating the results of critical thinking' (ibid.). This critical thinking about how to communicate written results effectively definitely ties into the research process when student assignments require outside sources to be consulted in the writing process.

As Jonathan Hall (2005) writes:

> Student plagiarism occurs in all academic disciplines, and so, for those of us involved with Writing Across the Curriculum and Writing In the Disciplines programs, the first thing we have to admit is: yes, it is our problem. It's everybody's problem, at bottom, of course, but WAC/WID directors are ideally positioned to offer both new conceptual perspectives and new practical initiatives: nobody else on campus is concerned with writing in every department and discipline, and at all levels. Faculty are going to look to us to provide campus leadership on the plagiarism issue, and we need to be ready both to present a more nuanced idea of what plagiarism is, and to develop a coordinated and effective campus-wide plan to address its underlying causes, and thus help to stop it before it happens.

Hall goes on to identify four pedagogical approaches that writing instructors should follow to help anti-plagiarism instructional efforts grow. One of his stated approaches involves working with librarians. Hall (ibid.) urges instructors to 'Get students involved in developing anti-plagiarism activities. Help faculty, administrators, librarians, and tutors understand the student experience of plagiarism and incorporate that perspective into their interactions.' In specifically addressing the roles that librarians can play, Hall (ibid.) states that success will be found in:

> activities that involve the library staff in training students not just to find sources, but to evaluate them for appropriateness for a given project, and to use

them effectively and honestly in their own arguments. Information literacy must be a core goal of all contemporary universities, and anti-plagiarism efforts need to be a key component of any such initiative.

As Barbara Fister (1992: 154) notes, 'Composition, the teaching of writing, has been around a long time, just as has library instruction. However, both fields have emerged as fields in their own right, as legitimate and serious endeavors, only relatively recently.' Fister goes on to show how both writing and bibliographic instruction emerged to new heights in the 1980s. She points out that:

> Both fields responded to a new diversity in student populations and expectations in the sixties and seventies, managed to achieve a place in the academic world – if not respectability – by the eighties, and are now exploring a wide range of possible theoretical frameworks in the eighties and nineties. (Ibid.)

What Fister is alluding to is the simultaneous emergence of two powerful areas of study within the fields of both composition and librarianship – namely WAC programming and the growth of information literacy from its bibliographic instruction beginnings.

Importantly, Fister also identifies the crux of the problem that both of these movements continue to face in terms of gaining interest and support from discipline faculty in creating curricular changes to deal with such problems as student plagiarism. She writes:

> Both fields deal with the teaching of skills rather than content, which makes us stepchildren in the academy

while making us innovators in pedagogy... We, more than other fields, attempt to view the academic. (Ibid.)

By explaining why both WAC programming and library instruction have been somewhat marginalized within academia, Fister (ibid.) nicely summarizes many of the same problems that continue to cloud the advancement of educating students more thoroughly in how to cite and synthesize the information they retrieve in the research process ethically, thereby avoiding instances of plagiarism. Like the curricula of WAC programs and information literacy, teaching the nuts and bolts of how and why to cite external information typically still falls into the categorization of process-side skills of learning rather than subject-based content knowledge. Therefore, since subject-based content knowledge is generally emphasized more and praised as integral to student learning in higher education curricula, skills like writing and how to carry out research are usually not a large focus of the undergraduate curriculum. Rather, they are often skills that many faculty members assume undergraduates should already have when entering higher education from high school, or should improve on by themselves.

Many recent and important studies on the intersection of writing programs and services and academic librarianship give greater credence to the idea that anti-plagiarism instruction belongs in the university curriculum, and particularly within information literacy instruction efforts. Focusing on how writing and information literacy efforts are linked, as they both stress critical thinking and active learning, Galvin (2006: 29) notes that:

The information literate person does more than execute a technically correct search and provide proper citations. The information literate person has to determine whether the information found is appropriate for his need. He needs to question whether sources are authoritative and timely. This dialogic approach to information requires the same active learning skills that are part of Writing Across the Curriculum.

Galvin emphasizes how important this connection is by citing how the Council of Writing Program Administrators (2000) 'issued a statement on desired outcomes which includes expectations that students will understand a writing assignment as a series of tasks, including finding, evaluating, analyzing, and synthesizing appropriate primary and secondary sources'. Other publications that solidify the importance of the relationship between WAC and information literacy include monographs like Elmborg and Hook (2005) *Centers for Learning: Writing Centers and Libraries in Collaboration* and Sheridan's (1995) *Writing-Across-the-Curriculum and the Academic Library* and articles such as Elmborg's (2003) 'Information literacy and writing across the curriculum: sharing the vision'.

Ironically, while many librarians and teaching faculty think that writing instructors are the sole members of the university staff working with students to prevent plagiarism, this is often not the case. As Galvin (2006: 31) notes:

> Writing instructors are not always aware of the similarities between WAC and information literacy. They tend to see 'library stuff' as a set of skills having to do with how to look things up, produce correct citations and avoid plagiarism. This 'library stuff' is seen as actually inhibiting active learning. Such

instructors believe that learning to use the library means that students will learn to gather information and 'dump' it back into their writing without thinking about it and incorporating the new information into their knowledge.

Clearly, collaboration between academic librarians and writing instructors is needed to clear up these misconceptions and fix real problems in information literacy approaches where they exist. Apparently, far too many individuals assume that someone else is teaching students about citation documentation styles and the ethical ways of incorporating external information into their writing – and this by and large is not the case.

A view of ourselves – a review of the literature

Reference librarians have probably helped track down plagiarized texts for patrons for centuries. Mentions of librarians working to help out in the detection of purloined texts can even be traced back to ancient times. As early as c. 284 BCE librarians like Zenodotus, the first head librarian at the Library of Alexandria in Egypt, and later Aristophanes of Byzantion were said to have developed systems and ways of tracking down evidence of plagiarism in the work of such writers as Menander (Long, 2001: 28). Detection and research to trace and/or document the suspected sources of plagiarized texts have typically been tasks that reference librarians have been requested to perform since then.

However, there are many times when librarians feel uneasiness about the role of playing a detective in light of our protection of library users' privacy. This is especially evident in cases where plagiarism is detected through interactions with students at the reference desk in academic libraries.

As John C. Swan (1982: 109) notes:

> There are situations in which, once again, personal judgment is all important in determining the ethics of privacy. A teacher who comes to the academic reference desk for help in tracking down suspected plagiarism has a right to expect it in determining which source a student was likely to use. But if the librarian had originally helped the student in question to his short cut, even unwittingly, he/she can be in an ethically ticklish position.

Similar examples of these kinds of awkward situations, where librarians find themselves ill-prepared to handle revealed instances of student plagiarism, were documented in the *Library Journal* case-study article entitled 'A lesson in plagiarism 101' (Anderson, 1994). This study, which was based on actual events, appeared in the 'How do you manage?' column to highlight how librarians are typically unfamiliar with their university's academic honor code and/or existing policies outlining how to handle and report detected instances of plagiarism. The article points out how library administration often fails to articulate clearly what the responsibilities of librarians are in working with students and faculty over issues regarding plagiarism, regardless of whether or not librarians have faculty status at their institutions.

The librarians depicted in the case study struggle with how they should deal with a case of plagiarism that a reference librarian uncovers during a reference desk interview. The profiled librarian had earlier aided the student, who has now clearly plagiarized, in locating the text in question. Now she has to determine if it is her role to report this case of plagiarism to the university or the faculty member. She seeks the advice of library management for a resolution to the awkward situation in which she finds herself. The case study reveals that librarians have not been adequately trained about their responsibilities in reporting instances of plagiarism. It is also evident that the role of the librarian in combating plagiarism is not clearly defined in the minds of the librarians involved in the case or in those of library administrators. Beyond these issues, the case study also highlights the instructional role that librarians can play in helping students understand what constitutes plagiarism and how to use information ethically.

This 1994 piece represents one of the earliest attempts within the library literature to address the awkward situation in which many librarians find themselves when trying to address plagiarism problems. Ironically, as librarians, our discomfort is not so different from the feelings that discipline teaching faculty express in terms of being misinformed or unaware of university policies on plagiarism.

I often use this case study as an icebreaker in the live online web seminar, 'The role of the librarian in combating student plagiarism', that I teach for the ACRL and during in-person workshops. In the case of the web seminar, enrolled participants are assigned to read the case study prior to the session. I then prompt them for their reactions to the piece at the start of the session. Despite the age of the article, by and large participants' reactions still mirror many of the situations and responses expressed in 1994.

The major difference between the participants' views and those of the librarians profiled in the 1994 piece usually stems from the fact that the majority of the participants are enrolled in the class to develop techniques to present instructional solutions to students to prevent plagiarism. The more reactive responses of the librarians profiled in the 1994 case study are realistically no longer completely acceptable for today's librarians engaged in information literacy instructional efforts. Past participants in the ACRL web seminars I have led since 2006 report both growing successes and trepidation at developing integrated anti-plagiarism strategies in information instruction, as well as excitement about the creation of drop-in workshops on citation style standards, bibliography formatting and tutorials geared for self-paced instruction.

Since the 1990s librarians have truly begun to grow into their role as teachers due to the growth of information literacy programming. Moreover, the instructional programs within which they work in their libraries are often replete with avenues for developing interesting and creative ways to engage students in the age-old topic of generating complete and accurate bibliographic citations for their research papers or projects. Going back a decade earlier, to the 1980s, scattered discussions about the possible roles that librarians can play in deterring student plagiarism also included such instructional solutions as providing assistance through the development of workbooks, tutorials and curricula.

Nevertheless, the 1994 *Library Journal* case study (ibid.) typifies early library literature coverage of the issue of plagiarism due to its focus on the librarian acting as a plagiarism-detection service rather than as an educator. Today's literature and research on the proactive roles that library instruction and reference services can play in collaboratively working with faculty and other partners to focus student attention on issues of academic integrity and plagiarism are somewhat more recent phenomena. In fact, only very recent discussions of the role of the librarian in combating student plagiarism have focused on the relationship between anti-plagiarism instruction and information literacy student learning outcomes within departmental and discipline-specific programmatic curricular goals.

Academic libraries and anti-plagiarism efforts

One of the most revealing and early discussions of the problematic interactions that most librarians face in terms of how they choose to integrate anti-plagiarism instruction into their teaching sessions came in Lorna Peterson's 1988 article entitled 'Teaching academic integrity: opportunities in bibliographic instruction'.

While writing a chapter on academic integrity (Lampert, 2008) for the ACRL's *Information Literacy Handbook* (Cox and Lindsay, 2008), and in other earlier writings (Lampert, 2004, 2006), I often cite Lorna Peterson's (1988) research on the roles that academic librarians can play in promoting awareness about issues of academic integrity. Peterson's article deserves recognition and praise as one of the first published works supporting the notion that librarians should integrate discussions of academic integrity standards into their library instruction sessions. The crux of Peterson's argument pushes librarians to move into this area of instruction. She also wants librarians to pay careful attention to explaining to discipline faculty and students how academic integrity issues are present throughout the research process – from the retrieval of information resources to the synthesis of these sources and a writer's own ideas in both the writing of a paper and its bibliography. As I have noted previously, in Peterson's view 'the predominant misconception that discipline faculty already introduce students to acceptable ethical academic behavior standards is one of the largest factors leading to the rise of academic dishonesty infractions. Therefore instruction on academic integrity should no longer be viewed as the sole instructional domain of discipline faculty' (Lampert, 2006). Much has been written about the power that collaborative interactions between librarians and discipline faculty can have in preparing instruction sessions or modules for students.

Examples of excellent studies on the benefits of collaborative partnerships between academic librarians and outside faculty can be found in the writings of Raspa and Ward (2000), Kraat (2005) and Rockman (2004). But more can be done than just tailoring the library session to the assignment and discrete course curricular learning objectives. Larger ethical concepts can also be introduced by librarians within college course curricula, to help students understand issues that they will face both within and outside of the university.

Much of the time the ethical issues of plagiarism and academic integrity are accreditation standards on which academic departments are looking for guidance, in terms of the best ways to introduce the subject within the time constraints of existing curricula.

Alice Trussell of Kansas State University reported at the International Association of Technological University Libraries (IATUL) conference in 2004 on her experience in working with engineering faculty facing new criteria from the Accreditation Board for Engineering and Technology (ABET) that included students demonstrating 'an understanding of ethical and professional responsibility'. Trussell (2004: 1–2) noted that the 'Ethical use of research and scholarly information is at the heart of library and information literacy training... [and that] the shift in ABET accreditation gives librarians an enhanced opportunity to partner with faculty... to document ethics instruction.' The success of projects like Trussell's shows that Peterson (1988: 175) was correct in arguing that it

> is evident that faculty must participate actively in imparting the concept of academic integrity... librarians in their role as teachers must participate as well. There should be no fear of treading on someone else's territory. Academic integrity is the soul of the college and university.

In the case of Trussell the fact that ABET, the accrediting body of the department and college she serves as an academic librarian, was now asking faculty to make sure that graduating students understood ethical information issues gave her the opportunity to work with students on citation and documentation style, information ethics and other information literacy issues. Trussell (2004: 2) rightly points out that while 'not all worldwide accrediting organizations are at this time codifying criteria for ethics instruction in accreditation... it is likely a movement that will be made'. Emerging accreditation student learning outcomes and standards are just one area of disciplinary concern that librarians interested in tackling the issue of combating student plagiarism through information literacy instruction should stay abreast of in terms of outreach and instructional planning. By not keeping up to date with faculty and students' discipline-based needs in documentation style requirements, accreditation standards and other issues, academic librarians will continue to miss opportunities to help students and faculty with an important component of the research process.

Peterson (1988: 168) clearly identifies where and how academic librarians typically fail to become involved in similar issues of academic integrity within library instruction:

> As participants in the scholarly process, librarians traditionally have seen their role as one of the teaching [of] the mechanics of identifying and locating books and articles; only occasionally does a BI program include the evaluation of such materials or the how-to of proper documentation. And, like the teaching faculty, librarians generally fail to address questions of academic integrity.

Since Peterson's article, which was written before the height of the information literacy movement, other researchers have also examined the need for librarians to approach issues of academic integrity actively in information literacy sessions. Studies such as those by Nicole J. Auer and Ellen M. Krupar (2001), D. Scott Brandt (2002) and Patti Schifter Caravello (2006) realize the unique role that librarians can play in working on issues of academic integrity by discussing issues of plagiarism with students at both the undergraduate and graduate levels. These studies rightly contend that librarians' in-depth knowledge of subjects such as copyright, intellectual property and research documentation styles make them ideal experts who should contribute to their university's education response to issues of academic integrity. Brandt (2002: 39) notes that:

> Issues related to copyright apply in a similar vein to plagiarism. In fact, copyright abuse and plagiarism are like two sides of a permission coin – on the one side,

people take without asking, and on the other side, people take without telling... Librarians have a special perspective on plagiarism. Some teachers will talk about it from an intellectual writing viewpoint, but we can address it from an applied and technological perspective. It's not enough to say 'don't do it.' You must emphasize how and why it takes place, and what needs to be done to prevent it. Librarians have done a great job championing copyright, and we can do likewise condemning plagiarism.

Recent examples of other studies that reflect on librarians' experiences in integrating anti-plagiarism instruction into information literacy programming include the author's own work (Lampert, 2004) examining how discipline-based librarian approaches to combating plagiarism and academic integrity issues better engage students. Other works that deserve notable attention include Jeff Liles and Michael Rozalski's (2004) analysis of how attention to instructional pedagogy improves the delivery of academic integrity issues within library instructional sessions, and the work of Pamela Jackson (2006), who examines the efficacy of anti-plagiarism instruction through the development and use of online learning modules implemented within the California State University system. Jackson's study specifically assesses undergraduate students' understandings of proper paraphrasing techniques through the use of an interactive web-based tutorial, 'Plagiarism: the crime of intellectual kidnapping'. Nicholas Tomaiuolo's (2007) article entitled 'Citations and aberrations' also urges librarians to face the issue of teaching the value of accurate citation practices in research to students.

How others view librarians as partners in fighting plagiarism

In an e-mail interview conducted with Donald McCabe, the founder of the Center for Academic Integrity and a renowned scholar on issues of plagiarism and academic integrity in higher education, I asked what role(s) he would like to see libraries, librarians and co-curricular staff play in creating a culture that helps better define and encourage academic integrity and the ethical usage of information. Dr McCabe (2006) states:

> I think libraries, etc. can make their major contribution through educational campaigns designed to help young people understand the 'proper' research uses of the Internet. They're going to use it no matter what, and that's a good thing, so we should teach them how to use it properly.

Many others have also expressed their interest in seeing librarians and libraries take a larger stance on the issue of student plagiarism in light of the increasing online resources that libraries provide via internet access. It is clear that in many circles the concept of the librarian as teacher is growing and becoming an accepted role outside the stacks.

Within the field of academic librarianship, the remit of reference and instructional services has expanded since the 1960s to include a teaching role for librarians. Along with the growth of this teaching role, largely through the emergence of bibliographic instruction programs, librarians have often been asked to help prepare students to conduct college-level research assignments. Examples of a collaborative pattern of communication about student citation behavior and the research process can be seen in articles documenting the relationships forged between libraries and English departments dating back to the early 1960s.

Early studies focusing on the roles librarians could play in working collaboratively with faculty to enhance student research skills and term-paper writing skills appeared in the library literature in the 1980s. Evan Farber's (1984) review of faculty's tradition of assigning term papers as an introduction to engaging students in library use and research skills was one of the earliest examinations of the challenges and opportunities that exist when librarians provide library instruction to assist students working on term-paper assignments. Farber points out that, in order to be effective from the vantage point of both professor and librarian, term papers need to be broken into stages that allow students to demonstrate the skills they are developing in the process of writing the papers. He also keenly notes that there are alternatives to the term paper that lend themselves to teaching students the fundamental documentation processes needed to complete a lengthy paper, such as the annotated bibliography. While concerns about student plagiarism were not mentioned in Farber's examination of the benefits of presenting alternative assignments to the traditional term paper, he effectively cites Harry N. Rivlin's study examining the shortcomings of term-paper assignments. Rivlin (1942: 319) made an observation that many of us will still find compelling today: 'the actual writing of the paper is the least valuable part of the entire undertaking... What the substitute assignment should be will depend almost entirely on the nature of the course, the composition of the class, and the special needs to be met by the assignment.'

Clearly the process of developing a topic and finding resources to support research statements is often the more beneficial component of student term-paper or writing assignments. The key for librarians supporting these assignments through library instruction is to develop methods to help students deconstruct the processes that they will need to repeat in other research down the road. Proper understanding of citation standards and the value judgments that need to be made to determine how to incorporate outside material correctly and ethically into the text of one's paper is a critical component in which librarians can provide assistance.

Current and future roles for librarians

So what are some of the ways that I believe that librarians can currently work to help students and combat student plagiarism? Librarians can do some or all of the following.

- Work to promote awareness of citation and documentation across the disciplines by teaching style formats like MLA, APA, CSE, Chicago, Turabian, etc. Integrate discussions about plagiarism and citation behavior into in-class exercises and information literacy sessions where students are required to conduct research and write papers and reports using outside sources. Collaborate with discipline faculty and their departments to address and emphasize discipline- and field-specific standards and procedures for ethically citing information in written and other presented formats.

- Create webpages and online tutorials explaining plagiarism and proper citation and attribution techniques. By providing online help on how to avoid plagiarism with real student learning concerns taken into consideration, libraries are promoting an educational solution.

- Identify and work with campus partners (writing centers, tutorial centers, academic grievance boards, etc.) and departments to establish an academic integrity committee that develops programming and a repository for assignments and techniques that help to curtail student plagiarism and raise awareness about the importance of understanding documentation style variance throughout the disciplines.

- Help their libraries work to create and/or document plagiarism policies with campus partners to support institutional ethics and academic behavior policy efforts.

From the above recommendations, the last one, urging libraries and librarians to work collaboratively to create policies that outline both educational and administrative responses to plagiarism, is a key step to creating a campus culture that informs students of both the consequences of detected plagiarism and ways to learn how to cite information ethically and correctly in their work. A recent ACRL publication, *Library Plagiarism Policies* (Stepchyshyn and Nelson, 2007), offers several examples of how institutions have developed effective policies in these areas. This work contains survey results on how libraries and librarians view their roles in combating student plagiarism, as well as participating institution and library plagiarism policy documents from such schools as Lake Forest College in Illinois and the University of Maine at Farmington. Many of the examples provided in this publication offer clear and detailed guides of how librarians and library administrators have worked with collaborative partners to create policies and programs to try to thwart the rise of student plagiarism.

3

How do students and universities view plagiarism?

> I hold my hands up. I did plagiarize. But I always used the internet – cutting and pasting stuff and matching it with my own points. It's a technique I've used since I started the course and I never dreamt it was a problem... (Michael Gunn, University of Kent at Canterbury student, quoted in Staff and Agencies, 2004)
>
> I would stress that throughout their time at Kent, all students are given clear guidelines as well as practical advice and support as to what constitutes plagiarism. These spell it out that it is not acceptable under any circumstances. For example in the School of English, this information is provided in the faculty handbook and in the department's own handbook, both of which are issued to all students. (David Nightengale, vice chancellor of University of Kent at Canterbury, quoted in Staff and Agencies, 2004)

In 2004 Michael Gunn, an English major at the University of Kent at Canterbury, admitted that he plagiarized throughout his academic career. Gunn said he did not know that his 'cut-and-paste' techniques were a problem until just before graduation. Ultimately he sued the university for negligence, stating that it should bear the responsibility for not informing him of the problems in his research and writing at an earlier time. Gunn is reported as saying:

> I *can* see there is evidence I have gone against the rules, but they have taken all my money for three years and pulled me up the day before I finished. If they had pulled me up with my first essay at the beginning and warned me of the problems and consequences, it would be fair enough. But all my essays were handed back with good marks and no one spotted it. (BBC News, 2004)

It may seem a bit extraordinary that a student would sue his or her university for negligence on the basis of claiming that the faculty and administration did not inform and/or educate him/her about plagiarism and its dire consequences. However, the Gunn case does reveal some of the long-existing underlying tensions about academic integrity issues. Universities and colleges, and their faculty and administrators, have primarily been involved in handling issues of plagiarism in terms of detection and punishment. Students have typically played the role of the offender, intentionally or accidentally, often claiming unawareness of the rules and standards expected of them when it comes to documenting external information that they have incorporated into their own writing, research or other academic products. This chapter gives a brief overview of how universities and their students, all over the world, view the problem of plagiarism. In addition to providing data and statistics, it will review the higher education literature on the topic. The chapter also gives current examples of proactive measures that universities and their faculty are taking to help combat and deter student plagiarism and other breaches of academic integrity standards.

Recent trends and facts on student plagiarism in universities

In a study conducted by Donald McCabe (Rutgers, 2003), founder of the Center for Academic Integrity, it was reported that '38% of undergraduate students used the "cut & paste" method of Internet plagiarism one or more times in the past year and/or paraphrased or copied a few sentences to an entire paragraph without citing the source'. It is also important to note that in this same report, 44 per cent of the participants stated they did not consider cut-and-paste internet plagiarism to be cheating (ibid.). Considering the growth of the internet and its acceptance as a primary medium for research by students around the globe, the growth of internet plagiarism incidents is not surprising. According to a Pew internet study conducted in 2001, 754 online youths aged 12–17 and their parents reported that:

> [the] Internet is vital to completing school projects and has effectively replaced the library for a large number of online youth. 71% of students reported using the Internet as their primary source for their last major project, and they also said they frequently accessed online study aids like Sparknotes or CliffNotes. Beyond legitimate assistance with studies via websites, or email or Instant message communication with teachers, students also take advantage of the Internet to cheat, with 18% of students reporting knowing someone who used the Internet to do so. (Lenhart et al., 2001)

The Josephson Institute of Ethics (2006) reported that 'cheating in high schools continues to be rampant. A substantial majority (60%) cheated on a test during the past year... and one in three (33%) said they used the Internet to plagiarize an assignment.'

In light of this trend, and the growth of reported cases of internet cut-and-paste plagiarism occurring at younger age groups within education circles, Dominic A. Sisti, a 2004 Templeton Fellow with the Center for Academic Integrity, launched a detailed study of the problem of internet plagiarism among high school students, entitled 'Moral slippage: how do high school students "justify" internet plagiarism?'. In a summary of his project, Sisti accurately notes the ramifications that result from K–12 students' collective shift toward internet-dominated strategies when selecting the academic resources they rely on to complete research projects, and the correlation with faltering information literacy skills. Sisti notes that many of these students lack basic information literacy skills needed for library research. He writes:

> It is quite possible that most students now lack a fundamental knowledge of library based research methods, Congressional numbering or even the Dewey Decimal system. Use of these conventions of library science has been supplanted by the innovation of web based search engines like Google.com. Students no longer riffle through long drawers of index cards to find resources; or even run searches against databases on CD or tape. Rather, students are now able to instantaneously access millions upon millions of 'resources' with a few keystrokes and a click. This type of research, while haphazard, may in some cases be perfectly appropriate and ultimately helpful in

completing an assignment. The overwhelming accessibility of written work – at one time it was unimaginable that millions of documents on a single subject matter could be accessed in less than one second – has propelled plagiarism to the top of the list of academic integrity infractions. (Center for Academic Integrity, 2004)

Why is this the case? Is it the ease with which results can be procured by clicking and finding resources and then moving seamlessly into computerized word-processing programs? Or rather is it that the traditional research methods that used to be promoted in K–12, and even later in higher education, have become watered down or absent in curricular offerings due to the assumption that students can and will find everything online via a search engine?

Sisti's most recent research (2007), which was published in the journal *Ethics & Behavior*, provides a sound review of how scholars have typically researched academic dishonesty infractions among undergraduates since William Bowers's classic work, *Student Dishonesty and Its Control in College*. In 1964 Bowers conducted a large survey of deans, student advisors and student leaders to study the frequency and causes of undergraduate cheating and plagiarism. Since Bowers, studies conducted by McCabe (2001b), McCabe et al. (2002, 2003), Ashworth et al. (1997), Higbee and Thomas (2002) and Pino and Smith (2003) have investigated the problem of undergraduate plagiarism and cheating, including examining its causes and possible solutions to thwart the growth of academic dishonesty.

As I noted in my 2004 article, 'Integrating discipline-based anti-plagiarism instruction into the information literacy curriculum', substantial research has been conducted regarding academic dishonesty and plagiarism within the literature of higher education. A hallmark of plagiarism research is that the issues of plagiarism typically end up embedded under the larger categorization of academic dishonesty. Thus it is essential in a review of this literature to examine both plagiarism and academic dishonesty together, as the two are often conflated. Future researchers in these areas should note that:

> The literature covering academic dishonesty can be summarized into the following thematic discussions: definitions and types of academic dishonesty (Whitley and Keith-Spiegel 2002), explorations of who tends to commit acts of academic dishonesty and why (McCabe and Trevino 1997), and faculty, student, and institutional perceptions and responses to academic dishonesty (McCabe and Trevino 1993; Higbee and Thomas 2002; Pincus and Schmelkin 2003). (Lampert, 2004: 348)

Faculty perceptions, reactions and treatment of student plagiarism are also key indicators of how students will respond to educational programming to help stop academic dishonesty.

Faculty views of student plagiarism

The perception, from both within the literature and beyond, is that most faculty view instances of student plagiarism as both intentional and problematic. In addition it is often reported that when faculty uncover plagiarism in their students' work there is either little guidance on how to handle the situation or the student is clueless about what the policies are in terms of punishment. Many faculty members consider student plagiarism to be a serious violation of academic ethics. However, as Pincus and Schmelkin (2003) report, not all faculty members agree about how serious a plagiarism violation is in comparison to other academic dishonesty infractions.

For instance, in their research Pincus and Schmelkin (ibid.) report that many faculty view a false bibliography or a plagiarized statement as a lesser infraction than copying test score answers or stealing a test. Moreover, the authors state that faculty views on the dimensions of 'seriousness' in rating student ethical infractions varied greatly. The findings of their research indicated that 'there is a strong interplay between whether academically dishonest behaviors are seen as a major violation and the severity of the sanctions that should be imposed' (ibid.: 208). This point is important, as student awareness and perceptions of the consequences of plagiarism and other forms of academic dishonesty are critical factors in determing whether or not students commit these dishonest acts, either intentionally and unintentionally. As the research of Carter and Punyanunt-Carter (2007) reveals, the way that faculty address and treat the problem of plagiarism impacts how students react to both university and faculty standards.

Plagiarism policies and their marketing campaigns

As Higbee and Thomas (2002: 39) noted in their study on 'Student and faculty perceptions of behaviors that constitute cheating':

> In order to be successful in college, students must be knowledgeable about institutional policies pertaining

to academic honesty. In this era of high technology, collaborative learning, and businesses that sell lecture notes, some of the boundaries between academic honesty and dishonesty are no longer clear.

Perhaps it is with this kind of thought in mind that many universities and colleges around the globe are now conducting campaigns to inform enrolled students about their academic honesty and student behavior and ethics codes. In regards to existing policies against plagiarism, many institutions have joined forces with their academic libraries to publicize and educate students about their school's rules and regulations.

University plagiarism policies and the role of libraries

As John Walker (1998) stated in his article 'Student plagiarism in universities: what are we doing about it?', higher education institutions 'need to be more proactive in: developing strategies to raise student awareness of the unacceptability of student plagiarism; developing and enforcing policies aimed at controlling student plagiarism; and setting up programs to promote academic integrity'. For most institutions, in both North America and the UK, over the last decade or so this has meant that their administrators and faculty have either composed or refined academic ethics policies that outline their institutions' standards and regulations for dealing with unethical academic behavior such as plagiarism.

Institutional definitions and policies about plagiarism help both students and faculty understand what their university regards as both acceptable and unacceptable behavior. Sometimes these policies take the shape of a student code of conduct or an honor code. As the research of McCabe et al. (1999, 2002, 2003) shows, honor codes have often brought success to academic institutions seeking both clarification and a reduction in the number of cases of reported and detected plagiarism. A clear and well-publicized policy about the consequences of plagiarism also helps guide faculty searching for the appropriate ways to deal with students who plagiarize within their institution's culture and regulations. As Chris Park (2004: 294) noted in his research:

> An institutional approach to dealing with plagiarism by students should set plagiarism clearly into context as a breach of academic integrity, frame it as inappropriate and unacceptable behavior rather than criminalizing it, embed it into the academic rules and regulations and promote it throughout the institution. An enlightened and positive approach would place the emphasis on prevention and education, backed up by robust and transparent procedures for detecting and punishing plagiarism. If successful, such an approach would create a level playing field on which staff and students can operate, to the benefit of all stakeholders. The key criteria in evaluating the usefulness of such an institutional framework are transparency, appropriateness, fairness and consistency.

Park is describing what other researchers have begun to identify as the need for a campus-wide approach to combating plagiarism. As I have noted in other writings, the concept of a campus-wide approach requires institutions to create a policy that embraces appropriate, fair and consistent rules that both deter plagiarism and increase student knowledge about how to avoid committing plagiaristic acts. The institutional framework that Park wrote about in 2004 was described as a 'holistic approach' by Macdonald and Carroll (2006). By adopting a holistic approach to combating student plagiarism, Macdonald and Carroll (ibid.: 235) emphasize that institutional policies should not only be widely documented and practical, but also part of a campus-wide plan to ensure that 'students have the appropriate information and skills within the context of a scholarly/academic approach to learning'.

This holistic institutional approach also asks faculty and administrators to develop 'approaches to curriculum design and assessment that ensure that skills development is built in and that assessment does not encourage or reward plagiarism' (ibid.: 236). Macdonald and Carroll's definition of a holistic approach that 'recognizes the need for a shared responsibility between the student, staff and institution, supported by external quality agencies' (ibid.: 244) should certainly also include the active participation of the institution's library and librarians, who like other academic units support faculty and staff and therefore can aid in such a holistic institutional approach to combating student plagiarism (Lampert, 2008).

Library involvement in holistic approaches to combating plagiarism

So how can libraries and librarians contribute to this kind of holistic approach through educational activities and the promotion of institutional policies? Examples of proactive library activities are growing annually and evident globally.

As noted in the previous chapter, in 2007 the ACRL published Stepchyshyn and Nelson's *Library Plagiarism*

Policies. In this work the editors compiled numerous examples of institutional plagiarism policies and programs which libraries and librarians have promoted in an effort to educate both undergraduate and graduate students about plagiarism issues. In the examples showcased in the publication, the majority listed their university's official policy on plagiarism in their library documents on plagiarism and academic ethics standards for citation requirements.

Student information literacy skills and plagiarism trends

If librarians and academic libraries really take the time to study students, in particular undergraduates, they will find there are many surprises about how they approach the research process. As the recent research edited by Foster and Gibbons (2007) shows, studying student behavior and practices reveals a great deal about what a student-centered library would need to do to help students working on undergraduate curriculum and research projects. In relation to the issue of student research and citation habits, some of the critical steps that Foster and Gibbons (ibid.: 80) identified as being used by four of the sampled students in their ethnographic study included:

> Gathering resources through the library, Google, professors or instructor, friends and family and other sources;
> Creating a bibliography or an annotated bibliography... this may entail the use of RefWorks, EndNote or another digital bibliographic tool.

While we are not really given detailed insight into whether or not the four students struggled with these aspects of the research process, we are told that 'every student has a unique approach to writing papers... and that we would do better to understand our students' lives not in terms of our own college experiences but in terms of our own current lives' (ibid.: 81). The ways in which students learn about citation and what constitutes plagiarism have changed greatly from when most librarians were undergraduates or even high school students. As Jude Carroll (2002: 39) reminds educators practicing in the UK, it is imperative that we think about 'where and when [our] students find out about plagiarism'. We have to see if their perceptions and understandings are misguided, and how they were established and reinforced in the first place. We also need to see if there are correlations between student information literacy skill levels, student perceptions about plagiarism and working knowledge of citation practices for research projects. The next chapter will discuss how developing information literacy frameworks and conducting assessment can aid in the development of student anti-plagiarism curricular programming.

4

Information literacy frameworks: working towards the ethical use of information by students

> Information literacy (IL)... is not restricted to library instruction resources or holdings; it presupposes the acquisition of the technical skills needed to access digital information, and crucially extends beyond the ability to locate information simply to include the ability to understand it, evaluate it, and use it appropriately. (Grafstein, 2002: 198)
>
> Although plagiarism is hardly a recent problem, the new technologies that render information literacy a timely and relevant interest also make plagiarism a pressing concern. (Norgaard, 2004: 223)

What does anti-plagiarism instruction have to do with information literacy programming? Is there a connection between the concept of information literacy and teaching students about how to avoid plagiarism by providing instruction in proper citation methods and standards? As earlier chapters have explained, there are educators and librarians on both sides of the fence on this issue. For the most part, the degree to which they disagree comes down to the question of who should be responsible for teaching the material needed to emphasize the proper usage of external information. In short, there are some librarians and other educators who would posit that it is the responsibility of the students to inform themselves about proper citation methods expected in the research process. Others maintain that writing instructors, from high school to college, have the sole responsibility for teaching students about citation and proper synthesis of materials gleaned from retrieved research. For myself and others, the role of information literacy instruction clearly encompasses these aspects of the research process, and therefore academic librarians can also be part of the educational solution to the growing problem of student plagiarism.

This chapter explores how information literacy frameworks and practices provide guidance and support for those working towards educating students about the ethical use of information through anti-plagiarism instructional techniques. The chapter will provide a background on how national and international information literacy standards identify instructional responsibilities in the area of teaching students about the ethical usage of information. In addition, a discussion of the theories supporting this area of research skills instruction is covered. Types of instructional delivery and curricular approaches that effectively support the adoption of anti-plagiarism instruction into information literacy programming will also be introduced to the reader.

Definitions of information literacy

Many researchers (Grafstein, 2002; Behrens, 1994) place the emergence of the term 'information literacy' around 1974. As Sarah McDaniel (2007) explains in her exploration of the conceptual models and practices that comprise information literacy, its momentum as a national and international educational movement began in the late 1980s, largely through the work of the ALA (see American Library Association, 1989) and the ALA's higher education division, the ACRL, which concentrated on developing standards for the application of information literacy curricular goals within colleges and universities.

The ACRL's *Information Literacy Competency Standards for Higher Education* document was developed by the turn of the century (Association of College and Research Libraries, 2000). These standards are now internationally recognized in the form of six student information literacy learning standards which are widely regarded as the foundational components of information literacy programming goals. In fact these standards are so well respected that it is common to see universities and colleges adopting student learning outcomes and assessment plans that relate to the ACRL information literacy standards in a lock-step fashion.

The ACRL *Information Literacy Competency Standards for Higher Education* state that:

> An information literate individual is able to:
>
> - Determine the extent of information needed
> - Access the needed information effectively and efficiently

- Evaluate information and its sources critically

- Incorporate selected information into one's knowledge base

- Use information effectively to accomplish a specific purpose

- Understand the economic, legal, and social issues surrounding the use of information, and access and use information ethically and legally. (Ibid.: 2–3)

These standards are then further broken down into 22 performance indicators, which contain student learning outcomes outlining assessable behaviors and skills that an information-literate student could be asked to demonstrate.

In terms of discussions pertaining to plagiarism and the ethical usage of information, the final information literacy standard, which states that information-literate students should be able to 'Understand the economic, legal, and social issues surrounding the use of information, and access and use information ethically and legally' (ibid.), provides the greatest foundation for exploring and developing anti-plagiarism and information ethics curricula.

In addition, the fourth learning outcome of the ACRL IL standards, which states that the information-literate individual will be able to incorporate selected information into personal knowledge, also has a related published-learning indicator: the information-literate student successfully 'integrates the new and prior information including quotations and paraphrasings in a manner that supports the purposes of the product or performance' (ibid.).

These structural underpinnings provide supportive and strong foundations for academic librarians and libraries interested in pursuing the integration of anti-plagiarism instruction into existing or developing information literacy curricular efforts. However, it is imperative to realize that having structural foundations is not enough to build a meaningful anti-plagiarism culture and curriculum successfully within an information literacy instructional program or classroom setting.

As Carol Kuhlthau (2004a) has stated:

> Although the [ACRL] standards are useful for defining information literacy, as specific objectives for instruction they may not accomplish the intended purpose of developing information literate students. Engaging students in inquiry that embeds information literacy in authentic learning may be more helpful for preparing them to apply knowledge to the information tasks in their lives.

Kuhlthau is widely respected for her writing and research on what she frames as the information search process (ISP), and for the ISP model of affective, cognitive and physical aspects in six stages of information seeking and use. While hearing her speak at the 2004 LOEX Conference, 'Library Instruction: Restating the Need, Refocusing the Response', I was taken with her recommendation that academic librarians search for what she coined the 'zone of intervention' during instructional moments. Kuhlthau's 'zone of intervention' presumes that there is a way for a librarian or other teacher to determine when it is important to intervene and when intervention is unnecessary in the research process. In her talk at the conference, Kuhlthau (2004b) urged instruction librarians to consider two critical issues.

- What is the zone of intervention that is helpful to an individual in his or her information-seeking process and after?

- How should librarians go about diagnosing student research problems and developing appropriate interventions?

In developing a response to the first question I began to ponder which 'zones of intervention' I typically worked on with students and faculty in my formal information literacy sessions and at the reference desk. The one glaring gap which immediately came to mind was that at the reference desk students presented many more questions about citation styles and research style standards in comparison to their queries posed during IL classroom sessions. I wondered why this was happening, and consulted colleagues to ask if they noticed the same trends in their interactions with students.

Overwhelmingly, many colleagues' experiences, both within and outside my own institution, supported my observation that students were very confused and anxious about how to integrate and cite external information in their research papers. In addition, it was clear that some students feel comfortable approaching a librarian with uncertainties about their 'citation problems', as they rightly consider these questions to be both a part and an extension of their research process. But it is important to note that those students who do come into the library for help are likely just a small percentage of a larger number who remain troubled or ignorant about how to cite ethically the external information they have utilized during their research.

As Kuhlthau (2004a) notes in *Seeking Meaning: A Process Approach to Library and Information Services*, there are affective, cognitive and physical tasks involved in the search process. Moreover, within each of the information search process tasks she identifies (initiation, selection, exploration, formulation, collection and presentation), levels of uncertainty arise and often prevent the student or researcher from moving forward or completing the research. The searcher's 'level of uncertainty' should be a key indicator to the librarian that the student is in need of assistance.

In addition to looking for 'zones of intervention', or as others sometimes call them 'teachable moments', it is also imperative when developing an information literacy curricular approach to help thwart student plagiarism to identify both partners and inhibitors to student success in this area of knowledge. For instance, is there clarity about where students can go for help through effective marketing of campus resources offering assistance in this area of the research process (library, writing center, office hours, etc.)? Have instructors and librarians begun to work collaboratively to identify problematic assignments or assignment redesigns that can benefit students in need of learning about how to avoid plagiarism? Is there a way to incorporate instructional time either within or outside the classroom to introduce the skills and concepts students need in order to 'integrate the new and prior information [they gleaned during their research] including quotations and paraphrasings in a manner that supports the purposes of the product or performance' (Association of College and Research Libraries, 2000)? Moreover, how should this instructional time best be designed and implemented? These questions require an analysis and breakdown of how library instruction and information literacy curricular programming are typically designed and delivered.

Information literacy instruction formats

There are many formats of library instruction, and their proper fit and success depend on proper planning, implementation and regular assessment. From the one-on-one instruction that takes place at the reference desk to the more formal classroom setting, whether it is a one-shot or semester-long course, there are numerous ways in which librarians reach students through their teaching efforts. While group classroom instruction is the most pervasive teaching modality, as Grassian and Kaplowitz (2001: 169) noted in a chapter aptly entitled 'The instructional menu': 'librarians are still planning and developing other forms of instruction, including "wayfinding" materials, standalone or supplementary aids, usage guides and practice materials, and other individual and group interactive modes'.

Many types of approaches to providing information literacy teaching have been identified in the literature of library and information science over the last 15 years. One of the most recent attempts to categorize these approaches appeared in an article authored by Li Wang. Wang (2008: 150) identified four broad categories that encapsulate the majority of instructional approaches employed by information literacy librarians and programs.

- *The intra-curricular approach*, where information literacy instruction is integrated into learning outcomes, activities and assessment in an existing course or academic program through collaborative efforts.

- *The inter-curricular approach*, where information literacy instruction is provided as an add-on session at the request of the course instructor.

- *The extra-curricular approach*, where information literacy is provided by the library outside an academic program and student attendance is voluntary.

- *The stand-alone approach*, where information literacy instruction takes place through a stand-alone curricular course dedicated to information literacy and/or research skills development.

While Wang's categorizations are useful and timely, for the purposes of deciding which modes of instruction might offer the best solution for developing anti-plagiarism or information ethics training, I will summarize Grassian and Kaplowitz's (2001) four categorizations of instructional modalities – in-person instruction, remote instruction, electronic/electric instruction and paper/other instruction – as I feel they offer more discrete examples of ways that IL programming can be achieved within the majority of existing library instruction programs.

In-person instruction

In-person instruction typically tends to take place either at the reference desk, via unscheduled drop-in sessions or scheduled office hours and/or pre-arranged appointments, or in the classroom or workshop setting.

- *One-on-one in-person instruction*. In the one-on-one type of setting, the advantage is that students receive personalized assistance that is tailored to their specific informational needs and research issues. The disadvantages are that this modality can be both time-consuming and imperfect in terms of its reach, as every student will not come in for one-on-one personalized assistance unless it is required.

- *Group in-person instruction.* As noted earlier, group in-person instruction is probably the most predominant instruction format currently offered in library instruction programming. Group instruction tends to take place in a classroom or computer laboratory setting. It usually occurs in a one-shot format, where the librarian only meets with a class for one session, typically ranging anywhere from 50 to 120 minutes in duration. Outside the one-shot model, other forms of group classroom instruction include drop-in workshop programming and the stand-alone semester-long credit course that is often run through academic libraries. Group in-person library instruction offers many advantages, including the ability to prepare and tailor sessions to course curricular goals, working collaboratively with teaching faculty to design a meaningful session, developing the opportunity for hands-on interaction and active learning, and cutting down on the repetition and volume that comes with a one-on-one approach. The disadvantages of the group in-person session typically arise when time is limited and/or the librarian does not feel s/he has the ability to cover areas of instruction that he or she believes would most benefit the students.

Remote instruction

Remote instruction has changed dramatically with the growth of the internet and web-based computer-aided instruction. Non-computerized types of remote instruction include one-on-one telephone instruction typically given through phone-mediated assistance offered via reference services. Workbooks and assignments delivered to the class without synchronous librarian mediation are other examples of remote instruction.

Electronic/computer-aided instruction

There are numerous modes of electronic or computerized library instruction now being utilized to deliver information literacy programming to students: static webpages; interactive web-based tutorials; integration into course and learning management systems (CMS/LMS) such as Blackboard, WebCT or Moodle; synchronous distance-education learning platforms such as Eluminate or WebX; and the development of virtual learning environments now being experimented with, such as Second Life.

In addition to these examples, instruction that takes place within reference services has also been drastically enhanced by the emergence of electronic and web-based software such as e-mail reference programs, instant messaging applets and synchronous virtual reference products like the OCLC's Question Point. Beyond all of these electronic additions to the instructional menu, libraries are now also beginning to experiment with utilizing and designing Web 2.0 instruction applications such as podcast recordings, screencasting and instructional blogs and wikis.

Paper and other forms of instruction

In addition to the creation of workbooks, paper formats of instruction include handouts, guides and bibliographies. Other formats are signage and the use of closed-circuit television and video sessions deployed via campus networks.

Other considerations

Of course, the above examples are not exhaustive of all of the types of instructional modalities that exist within the realm of library instruction. However, whether deciding to adopt any of the above approaches or another, it is imperative to consider the following issues, which may impact the success of your selections.

- *Staffing.* How many instructional librarians or staff members are available and/or needed to carry out successfully the preparation, development, delivery and assessment of the selected instruction mode?

- *Equipment.* What kinds of equipment are needed? Do you have enough classroom space, computers and classroom instructional technology devices (digital overhead projectors, audio speakers, DVD or video recorders/players) to deliver the instruction?

- *Preparation and training.* In terms of preparation, what kinds of computer software will you need to utilize and how difficult is it to learn how to use it? Consider that you may need web authoring software, image creation software, podcasting/screencasting and/or other audio/visual editing programs such as Camtasia or Captivate, Photoshop, Director, Flash, GarageBand... (the list can seem endless depending on what you decide to create to support instruction).

- *Time/budget.* How long will it take to develop the instructional curriculum and/or tools you decide to create? Do you have a budget for staffing, training and equipment needs?

- *Student skill levels.* What is the skill level of your target audience? How will you develop your IL curricula to target your various audiences effectively?

- *Assessment.* How will you be able to examine and/or show that your selected instructional modalities are successfully teaching students in the student learning outcome areas you have targeted and/or specifically designed your instructional sessions to meet?

- *Accessibility*. Have you taken into consideration whether or not the instructional modalities you plan to offer meet the needs of all students? Have you planned for students who may have physical disabilities that limit their ability to access material online? Have you collaborated with your campus center for student disabilities to learn the kinds of assisted technologies for which you should design electronic and remote instruction?

After analyzing the current needs and realities of your library's instructional program, the next step is to examine the content of the curriculum you wish to deliver. In the case of developing an anti-plagiarism curriculum, it is imperative to offer both practical and real-world situations to students in order to make the instructional content both interesting and relevant to their current and future studies. One way this can be achieved is by developing discipline-based approaches to delivering instruction aimed at preventing plagiarism and informing students about information ethics and standards in their chosen fields of study. The next chapter will examine how discipline-based approaches to combating student plagiarism are more effective and meaningful to students, instructional faculty and the librarians involved in developing this curriculum.

5

Discipline-based approaches to combating student plagiarism

One person's 'homage' is another's 'copyright infringement'. The question of originality in literature is complicated. Until the mid-18th century English writers did not hesitate to borrow from each other's work. Good writers, if they are honest, will acknowledge that when they come across a good thing in someone else's work, either consciously or unconsciously they store it away. (McCrum, 2006)

I have openly acknowledged my debt to her [Lucilla Andrews] in the author's note at the end of *Atonement*, and ever since on public platforms, where questions about research are almost as frequent as 'where do you get your ideas from?'. (McEwan, 2006)

Recent accusations and some proven cases of plagiarism or fraud in the literary world have reopened debates about how fictional and non-fictional writers, memoirists and such are supposed to document where they found background information during the course of their research. Within the USA and abroad, 2006 marked a year when it seemed at times that many authors, whether first-time novelists or seasoned writers, were coming under fire for either not acknowledging sources that served as inspiration or not acknowledging external sources or fabricated information.

Ian McEwan, the internationally acclaimed author of the Booker Prize-nominated novel *Atonement*, was accused of plagiarism in November 2006 (Volokh, 2006). McEwan, whose novel centers on the story of a nurse who tends to wounded British soldiers during the Second World War, was accused of too heavily using the memoirs of the late Lucilla Andrews as the basis for his fictional work without significant attribution. These accusations were quickly rebutted by the literary community in a series of letters and statements released by other well-known writers, such as Zadie Smith, Margaret Atwood, Kazuo Ishiguro, John Updike, Thomas Pychon and Thomas Keneally (Lyall, 2006).

In defense of McEwan, Thomas Keneally, the author of *Schindler's List*, was reported to have stated:

> 'If it is sufficient to point to a simultaneity of events to prove plagiarism, then we are all plagiarists, and Shakespeare is in big trouble from Petrarch, and Tolstoy stole the material for *War and Peace*... Fiction depends on a certain value-added quality created on top of the raw material, and that McEwan has added value beyond the original will, I believe, be richly demonstrated.' If not, Mr. Keneally added, 'God help us all.' (Ibid.)

McEwan successfully defended his use of Lucilla Andrews's autobiographical memoir *No Time for Romance*, stating that he had already repeatedly acknowledged using the memoir for research purposes and therefore was not guilty of any wrongdoing. Granted, all of this hubbub could just be chalked up as another fleeting, albeit interesting, case of well-known authors being accused of plagiarism. However, cases like McEwan's and that involving Dan Brown, the author of *The Da Vinci Code*, have caused many writers to begin the practice of placing bibliographies at the end of their fictional works in an effort to avoid uncomfortable scrutiny (Bosman, 2006b, 2007).

The purpose of this book is not to debate whether or not bibliographies belong in fictional works. However, the growing trend for novelists and other fictional writers to include bibliographies at the conclusions of their books has launched heated discussion within the literary and publishing world. Many experts are debating if the documentation of outside sources has and/or deserves a place in the field of literature and creative writing. The recent accusations of plagiarism and literary fraud have clearly ignited concern among writers and publishers wishing to avoid future claims against the ethical nature of their use of materials they uncovered through external research. *The New York Times* published an article discussing the decision that many novelists have made to include bibliographies in their works. As the article's author, Julie Bosman (2006b), notes:

> Traditionally confined to works of nonfiction, the bibliography has lately been creeping into novels, rankling critics who call it a pretentious extension of the acknowledgments page, which began appearing more than a decade ago and was roundly derided as the tacky literary equivalent of the Oscar speech. Purists contend that novelists have always done research, particularly in books like *Madame Bovary* that were inspired by real-life events, yet never felt a

bibliography was necessary... But some novelists defend the bibliography, pointing out that for writers who spend months or years doing research for historical novels, a list of sources is proof of labor and expertise. And it may protect them from accusations of sloppy sourcing in a climate fueled by lawsuits and plagiarism charges.

Discussions of whether or not bibliographies belong in fictional works may seem as if they do not pertain to the issues facing instruction librarians working on anti-plagiarism curriculum development – but they do. The emergence of a standard that expects bibliographies in fictional works represents an entry point for librarians in courses like creative writing and English composition. These disciplinary discussions, and others like them in other fields, signal a larger discussion of plagiarism's impact on the disciplinary cultures librarians serve. This chapter aims to continue our exploration of the librarian's role in discussing issues of academic integrity by showing how disparate disciplines and professions view acts of plagiarism differently, and how that can directly impact instructional work with students and faculty to combat student plagiarism. Continuing the examination of the role of anti-plagiarism instruction in information literacy instruction and librarian interactions with students and faculty, examples of case studies and methods will be provided for delivering a discipline-based approach to combating plagiarism through library liaison work. From my own experience, I believe these discussions are pivotal, as they open up important means for communication with faculty and students about how their discipline, or their prospective profession or field, views acts of plagiarism and the need to cite external information resources ethically.

An understanding of how different disciplines vary in their views on the ethical usage of information and the treatment of plagiarism is also essential for developing approaches to provide educational programming on these and other academic integrity issues on college and university campuses. These issues are also part of the larger need for students to become accustomed to academic culture and the practices of higher education, their disciplines and future careers, and publication and media standards.

Disciplinary approaches – a review of the literature

In my 2004 article 'Integrating discipline-based anti-plagiarism instruction into the information literacy curriculum', I explored how practical, discipline-based approaches to anti-plagiarism instruction can foster successful instructional connections between librarians and students and their teaching faculty (Lampert, 2004). The logical benefits of a librarian's adherence to a discipline-based approach to information literacy instruction are now better documented in the literature. Ann Grafstein (2002), the coordinator of library instruction at Hofstra University in New York, began the theoretical discussion of the value of a discipline-based approach to information literacy instruction.

As I have previously written, the strength of Grafstein's argument is that it sheds light on the fact that 'information literacy training outside of a discipline lacks the chance of catching student interest, as it will not be connected to assignments of progression in learning a discipline's required research skills' (Lampert, 2004: 348). As Graftstein (2002) also rightly points out in her argument for a discipline-based approach, a generic and somewhat gunshot approach to information literacy programming often weakens the ability of librarians and students to connect at a disciplinary level.

Grafstein (ibid.: 197) writes: 'Much of the IL literature emphasizes the teaching of generic skills related to the general process of retrieving and evaluating information, as opposed to the skills required for acquiring knowledge or doing research in a specific subject area.' She goes on to argue successfully that:

> imparting IL skills to students involves equipping them with both knowledge about the subject-specific content and research practices of particular disciplines, as well as the broader process-based principles of research and information retrieval that apply generally across disciplines. (Ibid.)

Some of Grafstein's motivation in arguing for a discipline-based approach appears to be fostered by the earlier ideas and writings of Stephen Plum (1984). Plum researched how the distinctive nature of disciplines impacts the way that students and researchers conduct research. He argues that effective library instruction must take into account the unique characteristics of disciplines and how research is conducted within them. Plum's (ibid.: 31) observation that disciplinary contexts are created by 'distinctive research processes of original research, literature structures and library systems' still holds true despite the growth of online research resources. A missing element of disciplinary approaches to information literacy instruction, which needs to be added to students' learning experiences, is the distinctive disciplinary nature of how researchers in a particular field synthesize and document the information that they obtain to inform their research findings. In his examination of the value of including instruction on documentation and the use of citations, Plum (ibid.: 29) writes:

> A course in bibliographic instruction should teach students a standard format for citation as well as the reasons for citing. Style manuals that specify standard formats for citations are often associated with particular disciplines. The reasons for and the uses of references vary widely among different areas of study.

Building on his earlier research with Topsy Smalley (Smalley and Plum, 1982), Plum (1984: 28) goes on to state that:

> Documentation in literary research enables the reader to identify sources and gives authority and credibility to the work. When to cite involves value judgment, and the use of citations can strengthen or disrupt an argument. Students should be encouraged to use citations creatively, even artistically. To teach judgment in literary research, students should be required to write selected, but not exhaustive bibliographies.

Certainly it seems hard to argue with the logic of Plum's observations. But why does a discipline-based approach to anti-plagiarism and academic integrity instruction have a greater impact than generalized instruction on these issues? I believe the answer lies in the unique learning experiences that disciplinary studies and research approaches offer students. While there are critical thinking skills that are required in covering generalized content about the ethical usage and documentation of retrieved information, there are also unique and specialized methods and standards that exist in every discipline's individual prescription of how to produce scholarship. Writing instructors and writing centers have long promoted the idea of disciplinary approaches to providing instruction about avoiding plagiarism and ethically citing information. As writing center instructors note at the University of Kansas:

> The tactics to avoid plagiarism are best taught in the individual disciplines. There, students can learn the relation of research to their writing in the particular discipline in which they are working and can be introduced to the conventions that will allow them to credit the origin of their information... even when the composition course does a careful job, that instruction must be reinforced by other courses before students will take the message to heart... Further, different disciplines follow different systems for making citations, reflecting not just differences in format, but also in the ways in which disciplines pose and solve problems and what they accept as 'common knowledge'. (University of Kansas Writing Center, 2007)

What do discipline-based approaches look like?

Once a librarian and/or faculty member is committed to approaching anti-plagiarism instruction from a disciplinary perspective it is not uncommon to hear the question: what would a discipline-based assignment or lecture look like? What makes it disciplinary in its nature? How does a disciplinary approach truly benefit students? In my experience, a disciplinary-based approach works to take the context of the discipline, major or field of study the student is working in and directly apply appropriate research skills and accepted scholarly and professional standards into the information literacy curriculum planning framework.

As Kate Manuel (2004: 281) has noted, the ACRL *Information Literacy Competency Standards for Higher Education* 'tend toward generality and universality... Disciplinary differences here are largely positioned as temporal, not fundamental.' Examining the standards closely, Manuel notes that the ACRL explains: 'Some disciplines may place greater emphasis on the mastery of competencies at certain points in the process, and therefore certain competencies would receive greater weight than others in any rubric for measurement' (Association of College and Research Libraries, 2000: 6).

Accepting the fact that information literacy standards and curricula have largely been planned for generalized implementation, it is imperative to remember and emphasize that disciplinary differences will emerge within disciplinary contexts; just as information literacy content should vary based on an audience and its skill level. In order to determine better how a discipline-based approach should be developed and taught, a librarian must work collaboratively with discipline faculty and observe how the field of study views the targeted IL skills in question. While Chapter 6 will go into further detail about librarian-faculty collaborations, the following ten points are critical to remember when working to develop and maintain discipline-based approaches to anti-plagiarism instruction in information literacy programming.

- Make sure to survey individual faculty and their departments about what citation standards they require from their students at both the undergraduate and graduate levels of study.

- Review the discipline-specific research methods that faculty members work to impart to students through their course content, assignments and syllabi.

- Routinely survey faculty to learn what areas of citation, bibliographic management and research their students are struggling with in their assignments.

- Ask faculty members how they feel they are preparing students working in their field who want to continue on for graduate work in the same field or an allied profession.

- Query faculty about what citation standards and practices are routinely required by their top disciplinary journals and associations.

- Survey faculty by discipline, department and college to learn if they follow and review university policies on plagiarism with their enrolled students.

- Ask faculty if they use Turnitin.com or other software to detect student plagiarism.

- Ask faculty to share any examples of how they approach the topic of plagiarism in their classes.

- Invite faculty to share information with you about cases of plagiarism, where appropriate, to learn what educational approaches might help alleviate these issues in future courses.

- Routinely review and inform both colleagues and faculty of news on how their professional associations and/or disciplinary accreditation bodies view issues of plagiarism and information ethics within their fields and professions.

Other tactics and approaches involved in getting anti-plagiarism instruction embedded into information literacy programming that are effective and meaningful to students require librarians to stay up to date with the pedagogical literature of the field of study in question. For example, it is very helpful routinely to review the literature of a particular field to see if researchers and instructors are publishing their approaches and/or research about student plagiarism within the fields where they provide instruction. A bibliography of examples of plagiarism literature organized by discipline is provided at the end of this book for your further review (see Appendix I).

Conclusion: from discipline-based approaches to enculturation into the academy

Understanding that disciplinary approaches to plagiarism work and engage students is only part of the process involved in understanding how to improve and/or provide anti-plagiarism instruction. It is also imperative that librarians understand and value their role as what Michelle Holschuh Simmons (2005) terms a 'disciplinary mediator'. But instruction librarians, and the faculty with whom they collaborate, must also work to develop students' understandings of why they are being asked to conduct their writing and research in specific formats and ways. As Shilpa Shanbhag (2007: 9) convincingly argues, there is an

> immediate need for information literacy proponents to conceptualize information literacy in broader terms of academic literacy, and think about ways in which to

support students with a range of academic abilities. Clearly, this also calls for aligning information literacy discourse with research on students' experiences in higher education and the cultural conflicts these educational experiences bring forth.

Shanbhag posits that the development of information literacy from a broadly skills-based approach to library instruction in the 1980s to today's process-based and critical thinking approach demands that instruction librarians vest more thought in their delivery of academic and scholarly content in considering the personalized habits and understandings of undergraduate and graduate knowledge levels. Shanbhag (ibid.: 9) states: 'We now know that students as learners need to see contextual relevance (personal, process, social etc.) of their learning, yet we are unable to provide much of a context other than that of a research topic or theme.'

Clearly, as this chapter has argued, part of the needed context in helping students become acculturated to the scholarly documentation practices of academe is to introduce and immerse them in appropriate disciplinary practices and views on the ethical use of information in research. In addition to providing that disciplinary context, which by and large is missing from the undergraduate experience, it is also important to make sure that library instruction as a whole corrects the problem that Shanbhag (ibid.: 3) exposes, namely that 'library instruction still largely remains divorced from the contexts that matter... [which include] the context of academic expectations and the context of student learning'.

Collaboration between academic instruction librarians and faculty interested in promoting an anti-plagiarism curriculum will be the key to melding contexts that have meaning to students from both the disciplinary and scholarly cultures needed for successful and ethical undergraduate writing and research practices. The next chapter will look at the necessary elements for successful faculty-librarian collaborations and other internal institutional partnerships to foster the growth of anti-plagiarism instruction and curriculum development across campus disciplines.

6

Thwarting student plagiarism through collaborations: faculty-librarian partnerships and beyond

After the internal commitment to the teaching role of librarians is established, we need to market our instructional role to the campus. This requires political skills... At the levels where curriculum is determined, the case for information literacy needs to be made. Deans and department heads must be convinced of three things: that students must learn how to access and use information; that these skills should be integrated across the disciplines; and that librarians working collaboratively with faculty are the appropriate instructional team to achieve that goal. (Caspers and Lenn, 2000: 151–2)

Student plagiarism is a much more complex issue than suggested by a one-solution response and this paper argues for a more holistic institutional approach that recognizes the need for a shared responsibility between the student, staff and institution, supported by external quality agencies. (Macdonald and Carroll, 2006)

Much has been written about collaborative partnerships and their relationship to successful information literacy programming. Collaboration between librarians, faculty and other support academic staff on college and university campuses is often the hallmark of productive programs that offer curricular solutions aimed at increasing student information literacy skills. This chapter gives an overview of what the literature has to say about the importance of collaborations between librarians and faculty and other academic staff. In specific relation to the issue of combating student plagiarism, the chapter will also offer suggestions of possible collaborative partnerships that readers should be able to forge in their own environments based on the literature, documented case studies and the author's own experiences.

Collaborative partnerships and information literacy programming

Out of all the books and articles written on the subject of collaboration and information literacy, Raspa and Ward's *The Collaborative Imperative: Librarians and Faculty Working Together in the Information Universe* (2000) is probably one of most respected and frequently cited in terms of defining how collaborative information literacy partnerships should operate. As Kendra Van Cleave (2007: 177) notes in her recent literature review on collaborative information literacy partnerships, Raspa and Ward differentiate collaboration from networking or coordination. Raspa and Ward (2000: 5) write that:

> Collaboration is a more pervasive, long-term relationship in which participants recognize common

goals and objectives, share more tasks, and participate in extensive planning and implementation... It is a more holistic experience in which we are committed to the enterprise, the relationship and the process.

In its *Characteristics of Programs of Information Literacy that Illustrate Best Practices: A Guideline*, the Association of College and Research Libraries (2003) lists collaboration as one of its key ingredients for achieving best practices in information literacy programming. The ACRL states that:

Collaboration among disciplinary faculty, librarians, and other program staff in an information literacy program:

- centers around enhanced student learning and the development of lifelong learning skills;
- engenders communication within the academic community to garner support for the program;
- results in a fusion of information literacy concepts and disciplinary content;
- identifies opportunities for achieving information literacy outcomes through course content and other learning experiences; and
- takes place at the planning stages, delivery, assessment of student learning, and evaluation and refinement of the program. (Ibid.)

Certainly all of the above characteristics of collaborative endeavors between librarians and partners are imperative for forming both lasting and productive partnerships. In addition to the listed characteristics, it is important to emphasize that librarians looking for collaborative partners must scan their environment in order to position their programmatic goals and strategies best within existing frameworks and curricula. In the context of collaborating with faculty and other academic staff to combat student plagiarism through curricular programming, it is critical to identify which parties have a shared interest in the problem of student plagiarism and academic integrity. For instance, depending on the academic environment and structure of the campus or university, those parties interested outside of the teaching faculty may include administrators, academic advisors, writing center staff, international student program administrators and student affairs officers.

Raspa and Ward (2000) are correct to differentiate networking or coordination from collaboration. However, in libraries, both academic and K–12, effective collaborative efforts still require elements of networking and coordination of staff, programs and services. In much of the USA, in the past 15 years or more the implementation of liaison programs within academic librarians has helped librarians establish long-term collaborative partnerships with departments, their faculty and other academic staff. An effective liaison program promotes collaboration by continually keeping lines of communication open for both the departments served and the library.

Examples of stellar library liaison programs include the University of Connecticut Libraries. They market their liaison program through their library webpages, where they explicitly list and define the liaison standards and responsibilities established by the University Libraries' administration and staff in 1989. In describing their academic liaison program, the University of Connecticut Libraries (2007) explain that:

> The program has built strong communication channels between the library and academic departments,

provided a framework for extensive collaboration between the library and the faculty, provided a mechanism for incorporating information literacy directly into academic curricula and for managing change in scholarly communication systems. Today, liaison librarians have become integral members of their constituencies and are regularly called upon to take an active role in enhancing academic programs across the system.

Like many academic libraries that offer a liaison structure to departments and faculty, the University of Connecticut Libraries emphasize that liaison librarians serve assigned faculty, departments and other academic entities in the areas of communication about the library, collection development, user services and program evaluation and development. In the area of user services liaison work, which is where librarians working to forge partnerships to thwart student plagiarism usually find themselves situated, it is imperative that there is consistent communication and assessment of the curriculum and student information literacy needs being served in the assigned discipline or department.

Liaison programs like the one described above allow librarians, both seasoned and new, to establish connections to faculty through a formalized structure. Library administrations must work with university administrators to ensure that liaison work is both respected and valued as a service of the library available to all academic departments and other applicable student service offices and agencies. Once this framework is established, it lays the foundation for librarians to have regular lines of communication open to discuss academic issues like plagiarism and student information ethics, as well as other areas of research skills development. As the literature has shown (Auer and Krupar, 2001; Lampert, 2004; Burke, 2004; Jackson, 2005), liaison structures give librarians committed to working on the issue of plagiarism linkages to sufficient student information literacy skills to develop deep and better ties with faculty and other concerned campus parties.

In 'Deterring plagiarism: a new role for librarians', Margaret Burke (2004) reports that librarians at the Joan and Donald E. Axinn Library at Hofstra University who are interested in working on the problem of student plagiarism:

> have the chance to become trailblazers in educating students on the proper methods for conducting research in the current electronic environment. At Hofstra we subscribe to over 100 online databases, many of them full-text, and yet often students still turn to the Internet as their primary research tool... In an effort to keep faculty up-to-date on all of our electronic databases and services, library liaisons have offered 'brown bag' sessions. Since it is not always convenient for the faculty to come to the library, library liaisons have gone to the departments, equipped with a laptop, to demonstrate how to access our databases. These brown bag sessions have proven to be very successful.

Burke (ibid.) goes on to discuss how librarians working within their existing liaison structure had the ability and positioning not only to provide instruction on databases but to respond to faculty and departmental concern over escalating student plagiarism reports by giving assistance on plagiarism-detection services, including both traditional reference detective work and later the adoption of the

Turnitin.com software. In addition to the traditional subject-specific curricular-based information literacy sessions offered at Hofstra's library, librarians also provide a one-unit credit course where they 'explain the research process, demonstrate how and when to cite sources... offer a detailed explanation of what constitutes plagiarism [and] describe how Turnitin.com functions' (ibid.).

Collaboration with faculty to create curricular solutions that help thwart the problem of student plagiarism requires both patience and constant communication about assignments and resources being used or recommended to students for their research needs. Moreover, collaboration to develop approaches for instructing students about plagiarism also requires intermediation through interactive information literacy instructional services, whether they are delivered through face-to-face instruction or online learning modules (tutorials, learning management systems, podcasts, etc.).

Looking beyond faculty – other possible collaborative partnerships

In addition to the connections that can be made between librarians and instructional faculty to thwart student plagiarism, a great deal of effective work can be achieved through partnerships with other campus entities. Examples of possible effective partners that librarians and others may want to explore within their own campus structures include writing centers, offices of international students, student services officers, student government and centers for faculty instructional/pedagogical development. Collaborative partnerships forged beyond faculty-librarian boundaries not only increase efforts but also market and cement the library's commitment to the issue of student plagiarism across the entire campus population.

Collaborations with writing centers

Much has been written and observed in the past decade about the value of forging partnerships between libraries and campus writing centers. As Elmborg and Hook (2005: 1) note, the timing for partnerships between libraries and writing centers is now ideal.

> For at least the last twenty years, writing centers and libraries have been living parallel lives, confronting many of the same problems and working out similar solutions, each in their own institutional contexts. During that time, they have both established a new kind of instructional practice within the context of a sometimes resistant academic culture, and in some cases, have become change agents on campuses, advocates for the importance of teaching and learning and for improving the educational experience of students... Having achieved a level of maturity and confidence, writing centers and libraries are now able to strike more coherent institutional partnerships.

As Barbara Fister (1995: 34) explains, the missions of instruction librarians, writing centers and writing instructors are very similar.

> These programs share so many characteristics that it is hard, in the abstract, to tell them apart. Both are attempts to infiltrate the curriculum with basic academic and lifelong learning skills and to embed

those skills meaningfully in the disciplines.

Both writing center staff and librarians typically reach students outside of the classroom setting through interactions that take place during tutoring sessions or one-on-one instruction at the reference desk. It is within the time-sensitive context of these teachable moments that the opportunities to analyze both in-process writing and research citation habits and skills emerge. Librarians and writing staff are also often better able to see how students work on assignments issued by faculty. If students are struggling with the research and/or writing components of an assignment, a librarian, writing tutor or counselor is likely to know about it before the professor.

As Larry Hardesty (1995) notes, the often-complicated process that takes place after a student problem with an assignment is identified requires both strong communication skills and diplomacy on the part of the librarian or writing center staff member dealing with the faculty member. However, this kind of communication and insight into student learning offers both the faculty member and partnering librarian or writing staff member a unique opportunity to assess what students are having difficulty with. Perhaps the student is confused about citation style formatting or in-text quotations? All these kinds of problems can lead to accidental plagiarism, and thus they require instructional intervention.

In addition to working collaboratively to learn more about student assignments and the problematic areas of student research and citation skills, libraries and writing centers can also work jointly to promote student awareness about these issues. Many times libraries and writing centers move to share physical space and hours, and to collaborate on handouts, websites and marketing of campus plagiarism policies. Examples of these kinds of collaborative partnerships can be found at the following institutions.

University of Maine at Farmington

The University of Maine at Farmington Writing Center and Mantor Library created a tutorial called *Synthesis: Using the Work of Others* that presents important information about plagiarism, documentation styles and requirements, and information literacy ethical issues, including copyright.

Project website: http://plagiarism.umf.maine.edu/.

Tufts University

The Research Paper Navigator learning module at Tufts University was developed at Tufts Tisch Library in collaboration with the first-year writing program and writing center. According to the document written for grant-support instructors from the university, the writing center and first-year writing program collaborated on the content and design of the interactive module, which was created to support the writing and research needs of Tufts undergraduates. The Research Paper Navigator is linked into course content through the campus learning management system (Blackboard), and aims to improve student information literacy and research skills by 'including information from the writing center and first-year writing programs in the research planner, [so] the student would be made aware of writing issues such as inadvertent plagiarism, developing arguments, or rewriting drafts' (Ammons et al., 2004: 2).

Project website: www.library.tufts.edu/researchpaper/.

Saint Louis University satellite writing center locations within libraries

The Saint Louis University Libraries and Student Educational Services relocated a writing center satellite location within the Pius XII Memorial Library to increase visibility and student usage. According to Gail M. Staines, assistant provost of University Libraries, 'This new space is more easily accessible for undergrads' (Saint Louis University Libraries, 2007).

Partnerships with international student offices

Much has been written about the problems that many international students encounter with plagiarism within universities and colleges in the USA (Park, 2004). While it is important to realize that international students do not plagiarize more than other students, many researchers have focused on the special needs of international visiting students. As Pamela Jackson (2005: 198) explains in her case study on a needs assessment conducted between the library and the office of international students at San José State University: 'Many authors [Robinson, 1992; Scollon, 1995; Pennycook, 1996; Badke, 2002] suggest that the concept of plagiarism is a Western academic value and is not always a strong part of the academic environment in other countries.' Jackson argues that collaborative partnerships between libraries and international student services on college and university campuses should focus on creating webpages and tutorials directed at imparting information to international students, collaborating with campus pre-college English as a second language institutes, and increasing outreach orientation efforts to international students.

Citing Baron and Strout-Dapaz (2001), Jackson explains it is also imperative that librarians and libraries creating services to reach international students should remember that:

> Handouts and training should not only teach international students about library services and resources. They should also provide information about: library terminology; organization of materials; source citation examples and academic honesty/ plagiarism policy; layout of the library; and most importantly where to go for help. (Baron and Strout-Dapaz, 2001: 320)

Possible entities to partner with to reach international students include offices of international student services, ESL and TESOL officers, international student dorms and international student associations and study-abroad offices. Examples of existing partnerships include the following.

Montgomery College, Maryland: seminar for international students

At Montgomery College in Maryland the university offers a semester-long orientation seminar for international students that, according the published course description:

> Includes study skills, academic regulations, the American educational system, individual educational and vocational goals, communication skills, and American customs. Especially intended for students during their initial semester of enrollment in conjunction with American language development course offerings. Two hours lecture/discussion each

week. 2 semester hours. (Montgomery College, 2007)

If your university or college offers a seminar or orientation session like this, collaboration through the library could prove beneficial.

Project website: www.montgomerycollege.edu/ Departments/FYE/syllabus104.html.

University of North Carolina at Chapel Hill Libraries international student library tutorial

This tutorial, which is geared toward graduate international students, aims to introduce students to the libraries at the University of North Carolina at Chapel Hill, American libraries and research conventions that typify study in the USA. The section entitled 'Using Information' provides international students with information on citation and documentation standards required for US research papers and projects.

Project website: www.lib.unc.edu/instruct/international/ index.html.

Collaborative partnerships with student services

Depending on how a university or college is organized and funded, student services officers and offices often handle issues related to academic integrity, and therefore plagiarism. Partnering with student services officers to promote campus academic integrity codes and policies is an effective way to reach out to students and faculty grappling with the issue of plagiarism. Recent articles and presentations have shed light on the positive aspects of librarian and student services collaborations (Walter and Eodice, 2007; Walter, 2006). Examples of effective library and student services partnerships to deal with the problem of student plagiarism include the following.

University of California Los Angeles

The University of California Los Angeles College Library partnered with Student Services to create a self-paced tutorial entitled *Carlos and Eddie's Guide to Bruin Success with Less Stress* and a workshop currently titled Citations 101, designed to provide additional education to those students who have been sanctioned by the Office of the Dean of Students for unintentional plagiarism. According to Swartz et al. (2007: 110), the 'College Library and the Office of the Dean of Students have collaborated to develop and implement two major educational resources to help UCLA students to understand issues surrounding academic integrity and the ethical, institutional, and legal issues involved in information use and access'. The first resource, an online, self-paced tutorial, covers 'intellectual property and copyright issues; legal and institutional issues related to file sharing and copyright; the proper attribution of sources in academic writing; strategies for managing time, research assignments, and the many resources available on campus to help students cope with stress, procrastination, and campus living; and academic integrity and UCLA policies' (ibid.: 114).

Project website: www.library.ucla.edu/bruinsuccess.

UCLA's other collaborative project between its libraries and student services involves the development of a workshop, currently titled Citations 101. According to Swartz et al. (ibid.), this workshop is designed to provide additional education to students who have been sanctioned by the Office of the Dean of Students for unintended plagiarism. According to the UCLA library newsletter, 'Citations 101 has been offered each quarter since fall 2004, the workshop is designed for undergraduate students who have been sanctioned by the University for plagiarism, yet is open to all interested students' (University of California Los Angeles Libraries, 2007). The workshop is co-taught by a librarian and a student services officer.

Citations 101 workshop outline: http://staff.library.ucla .edu/newsweb/news1040.htm.

Collaborative partnerships between libraries and student government

Many student government groups in colleges and universities around the globe are taking notice of the problem of student plagiarism and the growth of institutional reliance on detection software like Turnitin.com. Student government involvement in both the creation and the marketing of campus student honor codes is often a good way to gauge how engaged student government officers are to the issues surrounding student plagiarism and information ethics.

In addition to working with students through classes and one-on-one instruction, partnerships can be forged with student government associations. In 2007, when I was invited by the University of Northern Iowa (UNI) to conduct two campus-wide workshops on plagiarism, the UNI student government association supported these programs. As well as working on the construction of a new academic honor code, student government officers participated in the development of the workshop by taking an online survey and presenting their views on the problem of student plagiarism. Officers and representatives of the UNI student government also provided the student perspective on plagiarism and its relationship to credible student scholarship during the two sessions, through collaboration with the Rod Library at UNI. Video of these UNI workshops is held at the University of Northern Iowa (Lampert and Joseph, 2007).

Collaborative partnerships with centers for faculty instructional/pedagogical development

Collaborative partnerships between faculty development centers and libraries have long been touted as keys to both developing and improving information literacy programming efforts. Many centers for teaching and learning within colleges and universities frequently hold workshops on the issue of student plagiarism and how to design effective assignments that prevent plagiarism and academic dishonesty. Librarians and faculty often jointly develop these workshops and co-present strategies for working with students on the issue of plagiarism. An example of an outline that one library uses when collaborating with faculty through a faculty development workshop dedicated to the issue of plagiarism is available from the State University of New York at Plattsburgh (http://faculty.plattsburgh.edu/holly.hellerross/Plagiarism .htm).

* * *

The next chapter will discuss in greater detail how assignments and lectures can be specifically developed and delivered, both within and outside the library, to help deter student plagiarism.

7

Practical approaches to promoting citation methods and the ethical usage of information

The origins of plagiarism have as much to do with the assignments we set as with the ethics of our students. (Norgaard, 2004)

In the past, we have spent one class period per year explaining the consequences of plagiarism to our middle school and high school students, but we had never spent time teaching students what plagiarism is and how to avoid it. (Ladouceur and Giavannoni, 2006)

There are many times when librarians encounter students at the reference desk having problems with research assignments. It is common to see students struggle with developing a topic for a research paper or locating the perfect resources for their assignment. However, another set of questions that regularly arise at reference desks around the world emerges when students have to formulate a bibliography or works-cited list for references they used or consulted while writing or completing their projects. It is typical to see students confused with many aspects of citation and documentation. Part of the problem lies in their unfamiliarity with the different formatting styles assigned across the disciplines. Another aspect of their confusion is the fact that many students are no longer adept at the research process beyond placing keywords in a search engine query box.

From blogs to podcasts and online full-text articles, the abundance of different formats and types of information available online often causes problems in terms of the rules of documentation. Students also typically procrastinate, and place the least amount of importance on documenting the sources they consulted when working on a research assignment.

Readers of this book should keep in mind that while there are many students who are confused about how to cite information properly, there are even more students out there who have no idea why they need to cite the external information that they used at all. While it is tempting just to offer short workshops on citation formatting, this will not solve the problem for every student. As Russell Hunt (2002) sagely noted:

> Offering lessons and courses and workshops on 'avoiding plagiarism' – indeed, posing plagiarism as a problem at all – begins at the wrong end of the stick. It might usefully be analogized to looking for a good way to teach the infield fly rule to people who have no clear idea what baseball is.

In short, before leaping into designing workshops it is important to assess what students do and do not know about what constitutes plagiarism and proper citation documentation. This will help ensure that the techniques adopted by librarians and faculty in developing an educational approach to combating student plagiarism reach the largest possible target audience effectively.

This chapter summarizes techniques that can be used by both librarians and other educators to teach students how to avoid plagiarism through proper documentation techniques. It also reviews the research literature to provide readers with a broad sampling of how other educators approach the subject of information ethics and research documentation with students. Examples of potential assignments, lesson plan approaches and exercises will be presented.

Why assignment design matters

As a faculty member and librarian at California State University Northridge since 2001, I was not surprised to read the following quote from a colleague in the 17 June 2006 edition of the *Los Angeles Times*: "'It's so easy to cheat and steal from the Internet that I don't even assign papers anymore,' said Bobbie Eisenstock, an assistant professor of Journalism at California State Northridge. "I got tired of night after night checking for cheaters"' (Terril Jones, 2006). While there are certainly teachers out there who share the same sentiments as this professor, other college instructors and teachers in the K–12 levels are finding that the best way to prevent plagiarism in student papers and projects is to adjust lesson plans and assignments to help deter students from the common pitfalls that lead to academic dishonesty. As Robert A. Harris (2001: 43) notes when discussing the benefits of constructing assignments to prevent plagiarism:

> In combating plagiarism, methods of prevention should receive major emphasis. Detection and punishment are challenging and time consuming... On the other hand, prevention measures, if carefully applied, hold the hope for substantially reducing plagiarism in the first place.

Many academic librarians find that there are times when they are consulted about research assignments. Whether these opportunities arise from reactive or proactive instances, it is imperative that readers understand what elements lend themselves to assignments that work to reduce and/or prevent plagiarism. Recent research has shown that one of the most important elements in building effective 'anti-plagiarism' assignments is to design projects that require students to pay critical attention to the research process. Process-based assignments force students to consider the ways that they will manage and account for information sources in producing their work. These types of process-based assignments:

> Call for careful attention to information resources, skillful assessment of their authority and appropriateness, and active student involvement in the final shaping of the research content. Close attention to the research process will elevate not only student learning, but also the academic ethos. (Hurlbert et al., 2003: 41)

Whether undergraduate and graduate students are dealing with written or non-written research projects, they typically consult outside sources to buttress their knowledge of the subjects they are investigating. It is important for educators to realize that the sheer volume of researchable information available today poses confusion to the unprepared student. By requiring students to select carefully and think critically about consulted resources while researching projects, instructors are sending the message that both preparation and documentation of the research process are required parts of the assignment, along with the finished product.

Table 7.1 indicates the assignment characteristics that many authors and researchers have claimed reduce instances of student plagiarism in term papers. Table 7.2 presents the same characteristics relating to non-written assignments. By requiring students to show their work, just as a mathematics teacher requires proof of how one completed one's work, students are put on notice that accountability and ethics are course requirements. Of course, for the best results assignments and their elements listed in the tables should be supported by instructions in syllabi and lecture content about assignment expectations.

Many universities and K–12 institutions require instructors to go over academic honor codes with enrolled students. Often students are asked to sign statements that they will not plagiarize or cheat in their courses. In addition, at many colleges across the USA professors are required to reprint the university's policy on plagiarism and/or academic dishonesty in their course syllabus.

However, beyond these measures it is also imperative for instructors briefly to assess student experience with citation and documentation standards at the start of a semester. For instance, in a class of freshmen it will be useful to poll how many students have experience in using MLA or APA citation formatting. Assessments designed to reveal how many students understand when and why they should use quotations in the text of their written papers are invaluable tools. It is also a good idea to survey whether or not

Table 7.1   Written assignment techniques

Type of assignment	What instructors can do	Benefit for students
Term paper	Pre-select student topics Require all students to work on the same set of topics or one topic	Students realize that the instructor has an advantage in seeing trends in the papers, identifying plagiarized passages by their frequency
	Require specific types and numbers of resources be utilized and cited (e.g. 2–5 books, 5 peer-reviewed articles, 1 website)	Requires students to prove which resources they used in writing their papers
	Require an annotated bibliography of cited and/or consulted resources	Forces students to identify which resources they consulted and report critically on their resource selections
	Break writing assignments into drafts and pieces and require students to show evidence of the external works they are consulting (print-outs, photocopies)	Cuts down on procrastination by helping with student time management Forces students to identify and prove which sources they consulted

students are comfortable with documenting different types of information from both print and electronic format realms. Librarians can help instructors trying to design these types of assessments and lesson plans by supplying the latest information on research standards for various formats and offering insight into what types of information resources students are likely to find in the local library collection.

Table 7.2 Non-written assignment techniques

Type of assignment	What instructors can do	Benefit for students
Oral reports (speech and debate, PowerPoint presentations, poster sessions)	Pre-select student topics Require all students to work on the same set of topics or one topic	Students realize that the instructor has pre-existing knowledge of topics and sources, and may identify plagiarized presentations
	Require specific types and numbers of resources be utilized and cited within oral presentation (e.g. 2–5 books, 5 peer-reviewed articles, 1 website)	Requires students to prove which resources they used in preparing oral presentations
	Require an annotated bibliography of cited and/or consulted resources	Forces students to identify which resources they consulted and report critically on their resource selections
	Break oral assignments into drafts and pieces and require that students show evidence of the external works they are consulting (print-outs, photocopies) in preparation for their talks	Cuts down on procrastination by helping with student time management Forces students to identify and prove which sources they consulted

Lecturing about plagiarism in information literacy sessions

For librarians it is often difficult to find the proper timing and platform to discuss plagiarism. Without the benefit of a semester-long credit course focusing on information literacy, creating a space to discuss library skills or research methods can be challenging in terms of time management. After all, librarians are often only allocated one or two sessions in which to transmit information to students about the research process in relation to their assignments and the discipline they are studying.

Nevertheless, there are ways that librarians can discuss plagiarism and proper citation methods with students. As discussed in earlier chapters, by designing lectures that cover examples of how to cite and how to locate information on documenting sources, librarians serve as both an introduction and a reinforcement to the issue of student plagiarism.

Information literacy exercises and tactics that help fight plagiarism

In addition to working with faculty to design both written and non-written assignments that encourage student accountability and documentation for resources consulted during the research process, librarians can also discuss issues of plagiarism in one-shot instruction sessions. This type of session typically lasts anywhere from 50 to 75 minutes in duration, and can offer an introduction to the topic of student plagiarism and concepts needed to document consulted resources properly.

Some of the ways that librarians can effectively address these issues in one-shot information literacy sessions include the following.

- Using real-life high-profile cases of plagiarism from different disciplines as mock research topics to demonstrate search strategies during lectures.

- Asking students to complete an exercise where they retrieve citations and then place these in proper documentation format.

- Demonstrating how available full-text resources offer students the ability to export citations via e-mail in commonly known documentation standard formats (APA, MLA, Chicago, etc.).

- Urging and/or requiring students to keep a research log that chronicles what sources they consulted during their research on an assignment.

- Discussing and distributing campus policies and culture on student plagiarism.

- Discussing electronic detection services, such as Turnitin.com, and how they are used on campus to detect plagiarism.

- Demonstrating available campus subscription citation management software such as RefWorks or EndNote.

- Having students practice paraphrasing (see Barry, 2006).

- Providing instruction, via print or electronic handouts, on commonly assigned documentation styles across the disciplines.

- Asking students to see if they can identify plagiarism from sample writing passages (see Willmott and Harrison, 2003).

- Showing students how to locate style manuals currently held in the library's collection.

- Providing time for students to ask questions about their concerns over citation styles and/or how they can avoid plagiarism.

- Encouraging students to take advantage of on-campus offices that offer personalized instruction on writing and research techniques, such as a writing center.

- Encouraging students to contact librarians about all the above issues for consultation.

The role of technology in anti-plagiarism programming

While most of the focus of this chapter has been on assignment design and ways to address plagiarism and proper citation methods with students, it is important to realize that there are many existing technologies within libraries that also support student learning in the area of proper citation attribution.

Today many of the full-text and abstracting index services available through both K–12 and college and university library collections offer students the ability to e-mail and export citations in widely accepted research formats. It is common to see students' eyes light up at the apparent ease with which they can send themselves a copy of the full-text articles they wish to read for their research papers along with a pre-formatted citation in various standardized documentation formats, such as MLA, APA, Chicago or Turabian. The struggle for librarians is to get students to realize that there are often errors in these computer-generated citations. But the fact that these services exist, albeit sometimes imperfectly, opens up a teachable moment – a 'zone of intervention' to discuss the importance of proper documentation and care in checking for errors in citation.

In addition to the citation exportation features that are now commonly found in full-text databases, many college and university campuses are also purchasing subscriptions to bibliographic management software packages such as EndNote and RefWorks. In the USA these two citation management products are opening up new training opportunities for librarians and the faculty and students they serve.

While there are other popular products on the market, these two programs have gained popularity and recognition in library instruction programs, which often offer drop-in sessions and instruction on how to utilize the software in conjunction with library databases. The following chapter will discuss how citation management products and plagiarism-detection technologies can offer both educational and corrective tools for the anti-plagiarism programs that an institution chooses to launch.

8

Plagiarism-detection software services and other uses of technology to combat student plagiarism

> We must also be aware of the shortcomings of plagiarism detection services. They are a tool, a weapon, a deterrent. But they have to be used wisely, with an awareness of their shortcomings. The human element remains vital. (Royce, 2004: 30)
>
> If used, plagiarism-detection software should be only one part of an institution-wide initiative, with the onus on individual college teachers to attend to online plagiarism among their students. (Scanlon, 2003: 164)

When it comes to writing about the problem of student plagiarism on college and university campuses, a lot of attention has recently turned to technological solutions. Most of this heightened attention has been placed on plagiarism-detection services like Turnitin.com. However, there are other ways in which technology can actually assist in preventing student plagiarism beyond technological detection services. Certainly, subscription and home-grown institutional plagiarism-detection services rightly play an important role in deterring plagiarism and aiding faculty in its detection. However, they are only part of a possible solution that should involve incorporating other technological and non-technological options into the mix.

This chapter examines the role that popular and emerging technologies can play when employed to help thwart student plagiarism. Focus will be placed on plagiarism-detection software services, primarily Turnitin.com, reference and citation management software and its uses, and the role of embedding plagiarism tools like these in learning management systems and other commonly shared portals for student and faculty consumption.

Technology as a detection tool: plagiarism-detection software

Plagiarism-detection software has been a part of discussions about solving the problem of student plagiarism for well over a decade. While there are many products that have been marketed to and created by universities and researchers, Turnitin.com is probably the most widely recognized software in the market today. Founded by John Barrie, 'iParadigms, the company behind Turnitin.com, got its start in 1996, when a group of researchers at UC Berkeley created a series of computer programs to monitor the recycling of research papers in their large undergraduate classes' (Turnitin.com, 2007). Turnitin.com's notability grew out of its less obvious commercial beginnings from Plagiarism.org, a website dedicated to providing educators with information, tips and techniques for working with the problem of student plagiarism. Plagiarism.org still exists, but it is now more clearly a linked marketing component of the company website for Turnitin.com. While some faculty and librarians remain skeptical about the uses of Turnitin.com, there are many who see its value as a detection service that saves time and creates awareness of the fact that plagiarism can more easily be detected.

The Center for Educational Resources at Johns Hopkins University does a very complete job of both training and informing faculty about the pros and cons of using plagiarism-detection services like Turnitin.com. Its online tip sheet (Center for Educational Resources at Johns Hopkins University, 2006) warns faculty against making a snap decision that the software will single-handedly solve their student plagiarism problems. It writes:

> *Turnitin.com* is analogous to such software features as spell check and grammar check within word-processing environments – they are invaluable tools for writers, but they do not eliminate the need for proofreading. Similarly, *Turnitin.com* can be useful in deterring and detecting plagiarism, but it is not the single solution to the problem. Controlling plagiarism requires a comprehensive approach that includes a strong university ethics policy, forceful detection, and thorough, ongoing instruction in what constitutes plagiarism and how to avoid it.

As many other centers for faculty development and libraries responsible for running plagiarism-detection software across the USA note when working to educate faculty about this software, it does have limitations. The Bruce T. Halle Eastern Michigan University Library (2007) reminds faculty using the service on its plagiarism assessment service webpage that these limitations include the facts that:

- While Turnitin identifies textual overlap, it does not catch other types of academic dishonesty, e.g. invented bibliographic citations and factual content fabricated from the writer's imagination;

- While Turnitin includes content from ProQuest's proprietary databases, it does not include the digital content from all the other online services subscribed to by the EMU library (unless another Turnitin client submitted the text as their own);

- Turnitin does not catch copying from print sources (unless another Turnitin client has already digitized and submitted the text as their own).

Turnitin.com, like many other plagiarism-detection software services, also cannot do the following (Center for Educational Resources at John Hopkins University, 2006).

- Provide a judgment of plagiarism; it provides data. It uses a set of algorithms to match text and, based on the results, produces an originality report that shows the percentage of similar text and the source(s) of the match. But faculty must review and interpret the report.

- Differentiate between passages that are properly quoted and cited and those that are not – a match is a match. Again, faculty must review.

- Detect ideas taken from a source, and it can miss extensive paraphrasing or summaries.

What are the benefits of utilizing a plagiarism-detection software tool like Turnitin.com? Well, it saves faculty time by enabling them to be able to run students papers through a database and quickly get a snapshot of what plagiarism might be taking place. In addition, it covers more ground than faculty would be able to do by simply checking student writing against online search engines like Google.

Many faculty also report that it discourages student plagiarism and offers them some assurance that the university is working with faculty to try to detect academic dishonesty – rather them leaving them to their own devices to catch student plagiarists.

In addition to these benefits and limitations of Turnitin.com, it is also important to note that many students and faculty have launched considerable ethical criticism against the plagiarism-detection software service because it archives submitted student work in order to build its textual database. As Julie Rawe (2007) reports in *Time Magazine*:

> Every day more than 100,000 papers are fed into Turnitin.com, a plagiarism-detection site that compares each submission with billions of Web pages, tens of thousands of journals and periodicals and a growing archive of some 40 million student papers. More than 7,000 educational institutions use the system, including Harvard and Oxford. But while Turnitin lets faculty level the playing field, many students – even the straight arrows – see its use as a breach of trust.

The fact that Turnitin.com uses student papers to build its database has many students, parents and faculty crying foul. These critics claim that student rights are being violated in the process of trying to catch guilty students. In March 2007 Maria Glod of the *Washington Post* reported on how two high school students decided to sue iParadigms:

> The lawsuit, filed this week in U.S. District Court in Alexandria, seeks $900,000 in damages from the for-

profit service known as Turnitin. The service seeks to root out cheaters by comparing student term papers and essays against a database of more than 22 million student papers as well as online sources and electronic archives of journals. In the process, the student papers are added to the database.

The students' lawyer, Robert A. Vanderhye, was quoted as saying:

> All of these kids are essentially straight-A students, and they have no interest in plagiarizing... The problem with [Turnitin] is the archiving of the documents. They are violating a right these students have to be in control of their own property. (Ibid.)

For the moment, on most college and university campuses, student complaints about copyright and intellectual property infringements or other rights being violated by the institutional usage of Turnitin.com seem to be minimal. Earlier complaints about students unknowingly having their work entered into the Turnitin.com database have now subsided. Universities now seem to understand better the implications of their subscription to Turnitin.com in light of the US Family Educational Rights and Privacy Act. Under this Act, which bars colleges from releasing personal information about students without their consent, students in the USA should be made aware that their papers are being submitted to Turnitin.com. As reported in a 2002 *Chronicle of Higher Education* article focusing on the issue of student privacy rights and the plagiarism-detection software service, company founder Barrie acknowledged the issue of students' legal rights. He was reported as stating that:

As a result, the company encourages professors to warn students that copies of their papers will be checked and kept by the plagiarism-detection service, and to request that students themselves upload their work to the company's database. In that way, students cannot later argue that their papers were submitted to Turnitin.com without their knowledge. About 70 percent of the papers received by the service each day are uploaded by students, he adds. (Foster, 2002)

Certainly, there are still documented cases of students who refuse to sign release statements allowing faculty to run their papers through a plagiarism-detection database. There are also students who resent the idea that they are being presumed guilty of plagiarism by faculty who inform them that their papers will be run through the service. However, the usage of Turnitin.com is still very large, and reports of student dissatisfaction are growing quieter. Clearly, this is a technology that has its benefits and limitations. However, it does represent a powerful tool in the fight against student plagiarism, and it has also opened up faculty discussions about plagiarism issues on many campuses where only silence prevailed before. The important thing to remember is that education is still needed in addition to plagiarism-detection software tools. Students need instruction and repetitive practice on how to manage the external information resources that they consult during their research processes.

Reference and citation management software solutions

The existence of reference and citation management software that aids researchers in creating bibliographies and citations is nothing new in terms of the technologies that libraries and librarians are familiar with supporting or marketing. One need only review the literature to see the wide range of research that has been conducted on faculty reliance on products like EndNote (Walker et al., 2007; Koskinen, 2001; Brown, 1994) or the more recent interest in products like RefWorks.

As reported by Sue Koskinen (2001), EndNote, which has been available since 1987:

> Has the capability of connecting to online catalogs within the program, allows automatic downloading from Z39.50 databases (with the correct filter) and sorts by almost any field – date, source, author, title etc. It also is possible to create citations manually by typing each one into the database by field name or importing them from downloaded text files in online indexes and catalogs. Ultimately EndNote will save the user time, will make formatting papers simpler, and will ensure consistency across references.

Providing instruction to faculty and graduate students on how to utilize software like EndNote and RefWorks is nothing new to library instruction programs. In fact, the existence of such workshops and classes pre-dates the information literacy movement. Koskinen (ibid.) describes the robust instructional curriculum devoted to teaching EndNote at the University of California, Berkeley, as being open to both undergraduate and graduate students as well as faculty and the public:

> EndNote courses are offered by librarians every semester to users of all types: undergraduate and graduate students, faculty, and the public, including

government employees. Anyone who needs to manage information in a bibliographic format of almost any type can do so with EndNote... Students enjoy this class and are always impressed when the librarian accesses an online catalog within the program, performs a search, and downloads the citations directly into EndNote.

Today Thomson Scientific, the owner of EndNote, markets its product as:

A web-based tool for managing and citing references in papers and creating bibliographies. Integrated seamlessly with EndNote desktop and the ISI Web of Knowledge (SM) research platform, EndNote Web provides an online collaborative environment for existing EndNote users, and an entree for undergraduate students requiring a basic bibliographic solution. (EndNote.com, 2008)

EndNote typically finds greater loyalty among graduate students and faculty in terms of usage. RefWorks, another similar product, is enjoying a surge of popularity among undergraduate students and the librarians who work with them. As Ingrid Hendrix (2004) explained in a review of the RefWorks product (which has advanced a great deal since that time):

Its uniqueness lies in the fact that it is Web-based and is simple and easy to use. Because it is Web-based, users can access the program from any computer that has an Internet connection, and there is no local information technology support required, because there is no software to install or upgrade.

Many librarians who have taken my webcast course, offered through the ACRL, contend that RefWorks is an advanced online-only web-based citation management tool that undergraduates seem to be able to learn quickly and have great enthusiasm in using. In fact, the newest generations of researchers on college campuses appear to be embracing many of the online citation tools that some might have previously dismissed as unnecessary or tools for nerdy high-achieving students.

As Jane Kessler and Mary K. Van Ullen (2005: 310) report, due to the increased capabilities of citation management software and the growing student interest in its utility, librarians and libraries are working to promote RefWorks to their students: 'Now in addition to answering questions at the reference desk and teaching citation styles in information literacy courses, some librarians are offering classes [to undergraduates] on these products, linking them to style guide pages, and providing the software and instructions on library computers.'

Examples of libraries conducting these kinds of workshops and online help guides showing undergraduates how to use tools like EndNote and RefWorks can be readily found with any internet search engine. Many libraries utilize blogs and other social networking Web 2.0 tools to promote their campus and library subscriptions to tools like RefWorks. Some of the libraries currently offering workshops on RefWorks include:

- Dalhousie University (www.dalgrad.dal.ca.news/refworks06052007/);

- Colorado State University's Pueblo Library (http://csuplibrary.wordpress.com/2007/04/16/refworks-for-students-workshop/);

- Bucknell University (http://blogs.bucknell.edu/isr/2007/

03/students_refworks_can_help_you.html);

- San Diego State University (http://infodome.sdsu/ refworks/index.shtml).

Other unique marketing tools enlisted to promote subscription citation management tools include Arizona State University's (ASU) use of students in a video/commercial shown on its SDTV Library Channel and YouTube.com. The ASU Libraries sponsored video clip, 'RefWorks: The Ultimate Tool for Bibliographies', can be found at www.youtube.com/watch?v=OMFTvX%PqQ8 or through the ASU website.

Freely available tools like NoodleBib (www.noodletools .com/), EasyBib (www.easybib.com/) and other online citation-generation sites like Citation Machine (http://citationmachine.net/) and Style Wizard (www .stylewizard.com/) are also gaining tremendous popularity in the K–12 arenas, and therefore future college students will be familiar with or at least open to the idea of utilizing such tools in creating bibliographies.

But, as Kessler and Van Ullen (2005: 311) write, 'some librarians question whether students will ever learn to cite properly if they do not learn to do it manually first'.

While some may maintain that these tools are bad, as they give students a false sense of security that the computer-generated citations are error-free, I would contend that they are at least a step in the right direction. They hold the attention of students, who, like faculty, value the time-saving features they offer in terms of formatting. Moreover, the very databases that libraries spend large amounts of dollars subscribing to are already being programmed to export directly to commercial subscription citation management tools like EndNote, ProCite and RefWorks. It is not as if we can hide the existence of these tools. If anything, they provide librarians and libraries with a built-in citation development curriculum outline that can be the foundation for future workshops, webpages, tutorials and other learning modules. Like Turnitin.com, products like RefWorks can also be embedded into campus learning management systems (LMSs) to provide seamless reinforcement of course citation and attribution requirements and expectations.

Anti-plagiarism technologies and learning management systems

Recent reports in the literature and at professional conferences show that libraries and librarians are discovering great successes through embedded-librarian programs. What do we mean when we call someone an 'embedded librarian'? An embedded librarian is one who is attached to a course, typically through linkages provided in learning management systems such as WebCT or Blackboard. As explained by Ramsay and Kinnie (2006: 34–6), embedded librarians gain student trust in many of the same ways that librarians have always found via face-to-face interaction:

> We treat online students much the same as face-to-face students by offering instruction and providing direct reference help upon request. In WebCT, instruction takes the form of email messages to the class or discussion board postings that outline research strategies and appropriate sources timed to coincide with projects. When students are choosing topics for their research papers, a timely note on finding subject encyclopedias and using the catalog helps them locate material to develop their thesis statements. When

students need to find more current and focused information, the librarian posts a lesson on accessing journal articles. Reference questions are no different from those we get at the reference desk except they are asked and answered by email. It is not unusual for one student's reference question to turn into a lesson that can be posted for the entire class.

Embedded librarians and libraries that are linked into LMSs can also directly lead students into products like RefWorks. As Jody Fagan (2005), a librarian at James Madison University, reports: 'RefWorks is listed on the Blackboard "Tools" menu in all student and faculty courses. This is just an easy way to get to RefWorks from Blackboard... an instructor can create links to a specific RefWorks account, and this might be useful for sharing a reading list.' Cornell University has also integrated RefWorks into Blackboard for instructors, and reports that it is helpful in creating course reading lists and fostering group collaboration (Cornell University Library, 2007). Both these examples offer readers of this book ideas for how to market and use RefWorks in collaborative liaison settings with departments, faculty and students.

While anti-plagiarism technologies are clearly not flawless or perfected yet, they do offer additional tools that librarians and their institutions can experiment with in anti-plagiarism programming. The rise of Web 2.0 tools like blogs, wikis and podcasts also offers new opportunities for librarians and faculty interested in reaching out to educate students. The usefulness of staging virtual lectures (Guertin, 2005) to educate students on plagiarism is just one of the many paths that will hopefully be explored by more educators in the near future. Guertin (ibid.) defines virtual lectures as:

a product created by the instructor available to students outside of class at any time throughout the semester. Available for access through a variety of methods, the information delivered is consistent every time the student views the lecture. A virtual lecture can free up in-class time to cover discipline material and be available to any student that may have not yet signed into a course [at] the very beginning of a semester.

With the growing popularity of video downloads received on hand-held devices like cellphones and iPods or downloadable on to desktops, this additional way of reaching students, by either traditional or embedded librarians, would surely make an impact. As more technologies emerge and grow in popularity, there will undoubtedly be many new and creative ways to educate students via both library and university anti-plagiarism programming.

Conclusion

Writing a book on the issue of student plagiarism is not an easy task. There are many facets that one must consider and weigh. The focus of this book has been on the role that librarians and libraries can play, both alone and collaboratively, in working to educate students about how they can avoid plagiarism. By taking a look at the problems that exist within society and the status of how both students and faculty view plagiarism, I hope that at the conclusion of this book readers will feel they have gained both perspective and background on the issues we face. Plagiarism is not a new phenomenon. However, its prevalence has been enhanced by the growth of technologies that have created a culture where the lines of attribution, in the minds of students, are both blurred and slippery at best. Librarians, like other educators focused on process-based learning (such as writing across the curriculum instructors and other faculty), are in a unique position to impact student learning in this area of applied information ethics.

With our growing expertise and experience in creating effective and engaging information literacy programming, librarians and libraries can offer innovative solutions to the problem of student plagiarism.

The keys to success lie in locating practical and

meaningful solutions that resonate with both students and faculty, through both discipline-based and real-life examples that clarify why attribution and academic integrity are not only a crucial part of the educational process but also a necessity in the world beyond the ivory tower. It is the author's hope that readers of this book, regardless of whether or not they work in libraries, find ideas and concepts that will propel them to act, both individually and collaboratively, to identify and create proactive educational solutions to combat the problem of student plagiarism.

Appendix I: Discipline-specific examples of anti-plagiarism programming/pedagogy publications

Note: Please realize that this is not an exhaustive listing of all discipline/subject-specific literature on the topic.

Accounting

Abdolmohammadi, Mohammad J. and Baker, C. Richard (2007) 'The relationship between moral reasoning and plagiarism in accounting courses: a replication study', *Issues in Accounting Education*, 22(1): 45–56.

Anthropology

Gregor, T. and Gross, D. (2004) 'Guilt by association and the American Anthropological Association's investigation of *Darkness in El Dorado*', *American Anthropologist*, 106(4): 687–98.

Architecture

Alsop, Will (2002) 'Looks familiar… the perils of looking at students' work', *Architects' Journal*, 215(2): 18–19.

Buchanan, Peter (1996) 'Freedom of ideas under fire (architect Renzo Piano accused of plagiarism)', *Architects' Journal*, 204(10): 28–31.

Art history

Ashworth, P., Freewood, M. and MacDonald, R. (2003) 'The student lifeworld and the meanings of plagiarism', *Journal of Phenomenological Psychology*, 34(2): 257–78

Biology

LaFollette, Marcel C. (1992) *Stealing into Print: Fraud, Plagarism, and Misconduct in Scientific Publishing.* Berkeley, CA: University of California Press.

Willmott, C.J.R. and Harrison, T.M. (2003) 'An exercise to teach bioscience students about plagiarism', *Journal of Biological Education*, 37: 139–40.

Business

McCabe, Donald L. and Trevino, Linda Klebe (1995) 'Cheating among business students: a challenge for business leaders and educators', *Journal of Management Education*, 19: 205–18.

McLafferty, C.L. and Foust, K.M. (2004) 'Electronic plagiarism as a college instructor's nightmare – prevention and detection', *Journal of Education for Business*, 80(3): 186–9.

Chemistry

Del Carlo, D.I. and Bodner, G.M. (2004) 'Students' perceptions of academic dishonesty in the chemistry classroom laboratory', *Journal of Research in Science Teaching*, 41(1): 47–64.

Communications studies (public speaking)

Pearson, Judy C., Child, Jeffrey T., Mattern, Jody L. and Kahl, David Jr (2006) 'What are students being taught about ethics in public speaking textbooks?', *Communication Quarterly*, 54(4): 507–21.

Computer science

Dennis, L. (2004) 'Student attitudes to plagiarism and collusion within computer science', paper presented at Fourth Learning & Teaching Conference; available at: *www.cs.nott.ac.uk/~lad/work/portfolio/plagiarism.pdf* (accessed: 10 April 2008).

Engineering

Adeva, Juan Jose Garcia, Carroll, Nicholas L. and Calvo, Rafael A. (2006) 'Applying plagiarism detection to engineering education', in *Information Technology Based Higher Education and Training, 2006*, proceedings of ITHET Seventh International Conference, July.

Piscataway, NJ: IEEE, pp. 722–31.

Parameswaran, Ashvin and Poorima, Devi (2006) 'Student plagiarism and faculty responsibility in undergraduate engineering labs', *Higher Education Research and Development*, 25(3): 263–76.

Yeo, Shelly (2007) 'First year university science and engineering students' understanding of plagiarism', *Higher Education Research and Development*, 26(2): 199–216.

English

Wilhoit, Stephen (1994) 'Helping students avoid plagiarism', *College Teaching*, 42(4): 161–4.

Saalbach, R.P. (1970) 'Critical thinking and the problem of plagiarism', *College Composition and Communication*, 21(1): 45–7.

Geography

Burkill, S. and Abbey, C. (2004) 'Avoiding plagiarism', *Journal of Geography in Higher Education*, 28(3): 439–46.

History

Van Hartesveldt, Fred R. (1998) 'The undergraduate research paper and electronic resources: a cautionary tale', *Teaching History: A Journal of Methods*, 23(2): 51–9.

Mathematics

Rothstein, E. (2002) 'Plagiarism that doesn't add up', *New York Times*, 9 March, p. B9.

Music

Wakefield, Sarah R. (2006) 'Using music sampling to teach research skills: instructional note', *Teaching English in the Two-Year College*, 33(4): 357–60.

Nursing

Paterson, B., Taylor, L. and Usick, B. (2003) 'The construction of plagiarism in a school of nursing', *Learning in Health and Social Care*, 2(3): 147–58.

Philosophy

MacDonald Ross, G. (2004) 'Plagiarism in philosophy: prevention better than cure', *Discourse: Learning and Teaching in Philosophical and Religious Studies*, 3(2): 23–57.

Political science

Braumoeller, B.F. and Gaines, Brian J. (2001) 'Actions do speak louder than words: deterring plagiarism with the use of plagiarism-detection software', *PS: Political Science and Politics*, 34(4): 835–9.

Psychology

Roig, Miguel (1997) 'Can undergraduate students determine whether text has been plagiarized?', *Psychological Record*, 47(1): 113–23.

Standing, Lionel and Gorassini, Donald (1986) 'An evaluation of the Cloze procedure as a test for plagiarism', *Teaching of Psychology*, 13(3): 130–2.

Religious studies/theology

Phillips, Robert (2002) 'Plagiarism and theological education', *Journal of Religious & Theological Information*, 5(2): 3–12.

Shelley, Carter (2002) 'Preaching and plagiarism: a guide for introduction to preaching students', *Homiletic*, 27(2): 1–13.

Sociology

Abowitz, Deborah A. (1994) 'Developing awareness and use of library resources in undergraduate sociology: a sample assignment', *Teaching Sociology*, 22(1): 58–64.

Starfield, Sue (2002) 'I'm a second-language English speaker: negotiating writer identity and authority in Sociology One', *Journal of Language, Identity & Education*, 1(2): 121–40

References

ABC News (2004) *Primetime Live: Caught Cheating*, transcript, ABC News, 29 April.

American Library Association (1989) 'Presidential Committee on Information Literacy: final report'. Chicago: ALA.

Ammons, Elizabeth, Lowe, Carmen and Neatour, Anna (2004) 'Research paper planner: Berger proposal', March; available at: *www.library.tufts.edu/tisch/Berger/2004/ berger04_Neatrour.doc* (accessed: 25 February 2008).

Anderson, A.J. (1994) 'How do you manage? A lesson in plagiarism 101', *Library Journal*, 199(10): 80–4.

Ashworth, Peter, Bannister, Philip and Thorne, Pauline (1997) 'Guilty in whose eyes? University students' perceptions of cheating and plagiarism in academic work and assessment', *Studies in Higher Education*, 22(2): 187–203.

Association of College and Research Libraries (2000) *2000 Information Literacy Competency Standards for Higher Education*; available at: *www.ala.org/ala/acrl/ acrlstandards/informationliteracycompetency.htm* (accessed: 25 November 2007).

Association of College and Research Libraries (2003) *Characteristics of Programs of Information Literacy that*

Illustrate Best Practices: A Guideline. Chicago: ACRL; available at: *www.ala.org/ala/acrl/acrlstandards/ characteristics.cfm* (accessed: 28 January 2008).

Auer, Nicole J. and Krupar, Ellen M. (2001) 'Mouse click plagiarism: the role of technology in plagiarism and the librarian's role in combating it', *Library Trends*, 49(3): 415–32.

Badke, William (2002) 'International students in academic libraries: a user survey', *Academic Exchange Quarterly*, 6(4): 60–5.

Badke, William (2006) 'Teaching citation style', ILI Discussion Listserv; available at: *http://lists.ala .org/wws/arc/ili-l/2006-11/msg00257.html* (accessed: 26 February 2008).

Bailey, J. (2006) 'The "new" plagiarism', *Plagiarism Today* blog; available at: *www.plagiarismtoday.com/* (accessed: 28 January 2008).

Bain, Ken (2004) *What the Best College Teachers Do.* Cambridge, MA: Harvard University Press.

Bank, T. (2001) 'UCSB opts against plagiarism finder', *Daily Nexus*, 14 November; available at: *www .dailynexus.com/article.php?a=1792* (accessed: 25 February 2008).

Barlow, John (2006) 'I could have been a pretender: how I didn't end up like that Harvard sophomore accused of plagiarizing her novel', *Slate Magazine*, 26 April; available at: *www.slate.com/id/2140620/?nav=fo# ContinueArticle* (accessed: 25 February 2008).

Baron, S. and Strout-Dapaz, A. (2001) 'Communicating with and empowering international students with a library skills set', *Reference Services Review*, 24(4): 314–26.

Barry, Elaine S. (2006) 'Can paraphrasing practice help students define plagiarism?', *College Student Journal*,

40(2): 377–84.

BBC News (2004) '"Plagiarist" to sue university', 27 May; available at: *http://news.bbc.co.uk/2/hi/uk_news/education/3753065.stm* (accessed: 25 February 2008).

Behrens, Shirley J. (1994) 'A conceptual analysis and historical overview of information literacy', *College and Research Libraries*, 55(4): 309–22.

Bosman, Julie (2006a) 'Washington blogger quits after plagiarism accusations', *New York Times*, 25 March; available at: *www.nytimes.com/2006/03/25/business/25post.html* (accessed: 25 February 2008).

Bosman, Julie (2006b) 'Loved his new novel, and what a bibliography', *New York Times*, 5 December; available at: *www.nytimes.com/2006/12/05/books/05bibl.html* (accessed: 25 February 2008).

Bosman, Julie (2007) 'It's love at first cite: novelists tack on bibliographies to bolster the facts in their fiction', *South Florida Sun-Sentinel*, Broward Metro edition, 14 January, p. 7.

Bowers, William J. (1964) *Student Dishonesty and Its Control in College*. New York: Bureau of Applied Social Research, Columbia University.

Brandt, D. Scott (2002) 'Copyright's (not so) little cousin, plagiarism', *Computers in Libraries*, 22(5): 39–41.

Brown, C.C. (1994) 'Creating automated bibliographies using internet-accessible online library catalogs', *Database*, 17 (February): 67–71.

Bruce T. Halle Eastern Michigan University Library (2007) 'Plagiarism assessment service Turnitin.com', available at: *www.emich.edu/halle/turnitin.html#limitations* (accessed: 25 February 2008).

Burke, Margaret (2004) 'Deterring plagiarism: a new role for librarians', *Library Philosophy and Practice*, 6(2); available at: *www.webpages.uidaho.edu/~mbolin/*

burke.htm (accessed: 25 February 2008).

Callahan, David (2004) *The Cheating Culture: Why More Americans Are Doing Wrong to Get Ahead.* Orlando, FL: Harcourt.

Caravello, Patti Schifter (2006) 'Into the breach: teaching graduate students to avoid plagiarism', in Douglas Cook and Natasha Cooper (eds) *Teaching Information Literacy Skills to Social Science Students and Practitioners: A Casebook of Applications.* Chicago: ACRL, pp. 225–34.

Carroll, Jude (2002) *A Handbook for Deterring Plagiarism in Higher Education.* Oxford: Oxford Centre for Staff and Learning Development.

Carter, Stacy L. and Punyanunt-Carter, Narissa (2007) 'Acceptability of treatments for plagiarism', *College Student Journal*, 41(2): 336–41.

Caspers, J. and Lenn, K. (2000) 'The future of collaboration between librarians and teaching faculty', in Richard Raspa and Dane Ward (eds) *The Collaborative Imperative: Librarians and Faculty Working Together in the Information Universe.* Chicago: ACRL, pp. 148–54.

Center for Academic Integrity (2004) '2004 Templeton Research Fellows – Dominic Sisti'; available at: *www.academicintegrity.org/cai_research/templeton_sisti.php* (accessed: 23 October 2007).

Center for Academic Integrity (2005) 'New CAI research conducted by Donald McCabe', Center for Academic Integrity; available at: *www.academicintegrity.org/cai_research/index.php* (accessed: 25 March 2006).

Center for Educational Resources at Johns Hopkins University (2006) 'Deterring and detecting plagiarism with Turnitin.com'; available at: *www.cer.jhu.edu/presentations/tiitips.pdf* (accessed: 16 January 2008).

Center for Information Technology and Society (2007) 'How PAIRwise works at University of California Santa

Barbara'; available at: *www.pairwise.cits.ucsb.edu/ howitworks.htm* (accessed: 25 February 2008).

Cornell University Library (2007) 'Getting started with RefWorks in Blackboard – instructions for instructors'; available at: *www.library.cornell.edu/t/help/res_services/ bbrefworks-instructor.html* (accessed: 25 February 2008).

Council of Writing Program Administrators (2000) 'WPA outcomes statement for first-year composition adopted by the Council of Writing Program Administrators', April; available at: *www.wpacouncil.org/positions/outcomes .html* (accessed: 25 February 2008).

Cox, Christopher N. and Lindsay, Elizabeth Blakesley (eds) (2008) *Information Literacy Instruction Handbook*. Chicago: ACRL.

Crawley, Devin (2006) 'Citation sensation', *University Affairs/Affaires Universitaires*, December: 1–5.

Dames, Matthew (2006) 'Plagiarism: the new "piracy"', *Information Today*, 23(10): 21–2.

Elmborg, James K. (2003) 'Information literacy and writing across the curriculum: sharing the vision', *Reference Services Review*, 31(1): 68–80.

Elmborg, James K. and Hook, Sheril (2005) *Centers for Learning: Writing Centers and Libraries in Collaboration*, Publications in Librarianship, Vol. 58. Chicago: ACRL.

EndNote.com (2008) 'About us'; available at: *http:// endnote.com/enabout.asp* (accessed: 25 February 2008).

Fagan, Jody (2005) 'Integrating RefWorks and Blackboard', *Knowledge Edge (Online Newsletter of James Madison University Libraries)*; available at: *www.lib.jmu.edu/ edge/archives/Fall2005(1)/article3.aspx* (accessed: 25 February 2008).

Farber, Evan I. (1984) 'Alternatives to the term paper', in Thomas G. Kirk Jr (ed.) *Increasing the Teaching Role of*

Academic Libraries. San Francisco: Jossey-Bass, pp. 45–53.

Fister, Barbara (1992) 'Common ground: the composition/bibliographic instruction connection', in Thomas Kirk (ed.) *Academic Libraries: Achieving Excellence in Higher Education.* Chicago: ACRL, pp. 154–8.

Fister, Barbara (1995) 'Connected communities: encouraging dialogue between composition and bibliographic instruction', in Jean Sheridan (ed.) *Writing-Across-the-Curriculum and the Academic Library: A Guide for Librarians, Instructors and Writing Program Directors.* Westport, CT: Greenwood Press, pp. 33–52.

Foster, Andrea (2002) 'Plagiarism-detection tool creates legal quandary when professors send students' papers to a database, are copyrights violated?', *Chronicle of Higher Education*, 17 May; available at: *http://chronicle.com/free/v48/i36/36a03701.htm* (accessed: 25 February 2008).

Foster, Nancy Fried and Gibbons, Susan (eds) (2007) *Studying Students: The Undergraduate Research Project at the University of Rochester.* Chicago: ACRL.

Galvin, Jeanne (2006) 'Information literacy and integrative learning', *College & Undergraduate Libraries*, 13(3): 25–51.

Glod, Maria (2007) 'McLean students sue anti-cheating service', *Washington Post*, 29 March, p. B05.

Grafstein, Ann (2002) 'A discipline-based approach to information literacy', *Journal of Academic Librarianship*, 28(4): 197–204.

Grassian, Esther and Kaplowitz, Joan (2001) *Information Literacy Instruction: Theory and Practice.* New York: Neal Schuman.

Green, Morgan (2005) '"Cut and paste" essays get delete

treatment at UCSB', *Santa Barbara News Press*, 13 March; available at: *www.nmsl.cs.ucsb.edu/papers/cut-and-paste.pdf* (accessed: 25 February 2008).

Guardian Unlimited (2007) 'Mel Gibson being sued for plagiarism', *Guardian Unlimited UK*, 3 January.

Guertin, Laura (2005) 'Using virtual lectures to educate students on plagiarism', *First Monday*; available at: *www.firstmonday.org/ISSUES/issue10_9/guertin/* (accessed: 25 February 2008).

Hall, Jonathan (2005) 'Plagiarism across the curriculum: how academic communities can meet the challenge of the undocumented writer', *Across the Disciplines*, 2, 9 February; available at: *http://wac.colostate.edu/atd/articles/hall2005.cfm* (accessed: 25 February 2008).

Hardesty, Larry (1995) 'Faculty culture and bibliographic instruction: an exploratory analysis', *Library Trends*, 44: 339–67.

Harris, Robert A. (2001) *Plagiarism Handbook: Strategies for Preventing, Detecting, and Dealing with Plagiarism.* Los Angeles: Pyrczak Publishing.

Harvard Magazine (2006) '*Harvard Magazine* News Brevia', *Harvard Magazine*, September/October; available at: *http://harvardmagazine.com/2006/09/brevia.html* (accessed: 25 February 2008).

Hendrix, Ingrid C. (2004) 'RefWorks', software review, *Journal of the Medical Library Association*, 92(1): 111–13.

Higbee, Jeanne L. and Thomas, Pamela V. (2002) 'Student and faculty perceptions of behaviors that constitute cheating', *NASPA Journal*, 40(1): 39–52.

Hunt, Russell (2002) 'Four reasons to be happy about internet plagiarism', *Teaching Perspectives*, 5 (December): 1–5; available at: *www.stu.ca/~hunt/4reasons.htm* (accessed: 25 February 2008).

Hurlbert, J.M., Savidge, C.R. and Laudenslager, G.R. (2003) 'Process-based assignments: how promoting information literacy prevents plagiarism', *College & Undergraduate Libraries*, 10(1): 39–51.

ILI Discussion Listserv (2006) 'Teaching citation style mcnamal 11/28/2006', messages, 28 November; available at: *http://lists.ala.org/wws/arc/ili-l/2006-11/* (accessed: 25 February 2008).

Italie, Hillel (2006) 'Publisher cancels deal with new author', *Associated Press News Wire*, 2 May.

Jackson, Pamela A. (2005) 'Incoming international students and the library: a survey', *Reference Services Review*, 3(2): 197–209.

Jackson, Pamela A. (2006) 'Plagiarism instruction online: assessing undergraduate students' ability to avoid plagiarism', *College and Research Libraries*, 67(5): 418–28.

Jenkins, Henry (2006) *Convergence Culture: Where Old and New Media Collide*. New York: New York University.

Johnston, Bill and Webber, Sheila (2005) 'As we may think: information literacy as a discipline for the information age', *Research Strategies*, 20(3): 108–21.

Jones, Del (2006) 'Authorship gets lost on the web', *USA Today*, 1 August; available at: *www.usatoday.com/tech/news/2006-07-31-net-plagiarism_x.htm* (accessed: 25 February 2008).

Jones, Terril Yue (2006) 'If this were a term paper, you might have seen it on the web', *Los Angeles Times*, 17 June, sec. A1.

Josephson Institute of Ethics (2006) *Josephson Report Card on American Youth*. Los Angeles: Josephson Institute of Ethics; available at: *www.josephsoninstitute.org/pdf/ReportCard_press-release_2006-1015.pdf* (accessed: 25

January 2008).

Kessler, Jane and Van Ullen, Mary K. (2005) 'Citation generators: generating bibliographies for the next generation', *Journal of Academic Librarianship*, 31(4): 310–16.

Kirk, Thomas G. Jr (1995) 'Foreword', in Jean Sheridan (ed.) *Writing-Across-the-Curriculum and the Academic Library: A Guide for Librarians, Instructors, and Writing Program Directors*. Westport, CT: Greenwood Press, pp. viv–xi.

Kirsch, Jonathan (2007) 'To borrow a phrase... *The Little Book of Plagiarism*, Richard A. Posner', book review, *Los Angeles Times*, 28 January; available at: *www.calendarlive.com/books/bookreview/cl-bk-kirsch28jan28,0,5130367.htmlstory* (accessed: 24 March 2007).

Kleiner, Carolyn and Lord, Mary (1999) 'The cheating game', *US News & World Report*, 127(20): 54–63.

Koskinen, Sue (2001) 'From Colonel Mustard to Rube Goldberg: teaching patrons how to manage bibliographies with EndNote', *Art Documentation*, 20(1): 50–2.

Kraat, Susan B. (2005) *Relationships Between Teaching Faculty and Teaching Librarians*. Binghamton, NY: Haworth Information Press.

Kuhlthau, Carol (2004a) *Seeking Meaning: A Process Approach to Library and Information Services*, 2nd edn. Westport, CT: Libraries Unlimited.

Kuhlthau, Carol (2004b) 'Zones of intervention in the information search process: vital roles for librarians', paper presented at LOEX Conference, 'Library Instruction: Restating the Need, Refocusing the Response'; available at: *www.scils.rutgers.edu/~kuhlthau/recent_presentations/loex/loex_notes.htm* and *www.scils.rutgers.edu/~kuhlthau/recent_presentations/loe x/loex_presentation.ppt* (accessed: 21 December 2007).

Ladouceur, Andrea and Giovannoni, Marisa (2006) 'Teaching students about plagiarism using a WebQuest', *Learning and Leading with Technology*, 34(3): 34–5.

Lampert, Lynn D. (2004) 'Integrating discipline-based anti-plagiarism instruction into the information literacy curriculum', *Reference Services Review*, 32(4): 347–55.

Lampert, Lynn D. (2006) 'The instruction librarian's role in discussing issues of academic integrity', *LOEX Quarterly*, 32(4): 8–9.

Lampert, Lynn D. (2008) 'Student academic integrity', in Christopher Cox and Beth Lindsay (eds) *Information Literacy Instructional Handbook*. Chicago: ACRL, pp. 149–63.

Lampert, Lynn D. and Joseph, Sue (2007) *Techniques for Combating Student Plagiarism*, video of workshops conducted by Lynn D. Lampert. Cedar Falls: University of Northern Iowa Audio/Visual Productions Services.

Lenhart, Amanda and Madden, Mary (2005) *Teen Content Creators and Consumers: A Pew Internet Report*. Pew Internet & American Life Project; available at: *www .pewinternet.org/pdfs/PIP_Teens_Content_Creation.pdf* (accessed: 9 January 2008).

Lenhart, Amanda, Simon, Maya and Graziano, Mike (2001) *The Internet and Education: Findings of the Pew Internet & American Life Project*. Pew Internet & American Life Project; available at: *www.pewinternet .org/report_display.asp?r=39* (accessed: 26 February 2008).

Liles, Jeffrey A. and Rozalski, Michael E. (2004) 'It's a matter of style: a style manual workshops for preventing plagiarism', *College & Undergraduate Libraries*, 11(2): 91–101.

Long, Pamela O. (2001) *Openness, Secrecy, Authorship: Technical Arts and the Culture of Knowledge from Antiquity to the Renaissance.* Baltimore, MD: Johns Hopkins University Press.

Lorenzo, George, Oblinger, Diana and Dziuban, Charles (2006) 'How choice, co-creation, and culture are changing what it means to be net savvy', ELI Paper No. 4, Educause Learning Initiative; available at: *www.educause .edu/ir/library/pdf/ELI3008.pdf* (accessed: 25 February 2008).

Lyall, Sarah (2006) 'Novelists defend one of their own against a plagiarism charge in Britain', *New York Times*, 7 December; available at: *www.nytimes.com/2006/ 12/07/books/07pync.html* (accessed: 25 February 2008).

Macdonald, Ranald and Carroll, Jude (2006) 'Plagiarism – a complex issue requiring a holistic institutional approach', *Assessment & Evaluation in Higher Education*, 31(2): 233–45.

Manuel, Kate (2004) 'Generic and discipline-specific information literacy competencies: the case of the sciences', *Science & Technology Libraries*, 24(3/4): 279–308.

McCabe, Donald L. (2001a) 'Plagiarism and plagiarism detection go high tech: a *Chronicle of Higher Education* colloquy', transcript; available at: *http://chronicle .com/colloquylive/2001/07/cheat/* (accessed: 9 January 2008).

McCabe, Donald L. (2001b) 'Cheating: why students do it and how we can help them stop', *American Educator*, Winter: 38–43.

McCabe, Donald L. (2006) E-mail interview by author.

McCabe, Donald L. and Trevino, Linda Klebe (1993) 'Academic dishonesty: honor codes and other contextual influences', *Journal of Higher Education*, 64(5): 522–39.

McCabe, Donald L. and Trevino, Linda Klebe (1997) 'Individual and contextual influences on academic dishonesty: a multicampus investigation', *Research in Higher Education*, 38(3): 379–96.

McCabe, Donald L., Butterfield, Kenneth D. and Trevino, Linda Klebe (2003) 'Faculty and academic integrity: the influence of current honor codes and past honor code experiences', *Research in Higher Education*, 44(3): 367–85.

McCabe, Donald L., Trevino, Linda Klebe and Butterfield, Kenneth D. (1999) 'Academic integrity in honor code and non-honor code environments', *Journal of Higher Education*, 70(2): 211–34.

McCabe, Donald L., Trevino, Linda Klebe and Butterfield, Kenneth D. (2002) 'Honor codes and other contextual influences on academic integrity: a replication and extension to modified honor code settings', *Research in Higher Education*, 43(3): 357–78.

McCrum, Robert (2006) 'Warning: the words you are about to read may be stolen', *The Observer*, 3 December; available at: *http://books.guardian.co.uk/departments/generalfiction/story/0,,1962604,00.html#article_continue* (accessed: 25 February 2008).

McDaniel, Sarah (2007) 'Defining information literacy: conceptual models and practice', in Susan Curzon and Lynn Lampert (eds) *Proven Strategies for Building an Information Literacy Program*. New York: Neal Schuman, pp. 13–28.

McEwan, Ian (2006) 'An inspiration, yes. Did I copy from another author? No', *Guardian Unlimited UK*, 27 November; available at: *http://books.guardian.co.uk/comment/story/0,,1957845,00.html* (accessed: 25 February 2008).

Mehegan, David (2006) 'After duplicated words, words of

apology; Harvard writer says she "internalized" an earlier novel', *Boston Globe*, 25 April; available at: *www.boston.com/ae/books/articles/2006/04/25/after_dup licated_words_words_of_apology/* (accessed: 25 February 2008).

Montgomery College (2007) 'Seminar for international students'; available at: *www.montgomerycollege.edu/ Departments/FYE/syllabus104.html* (accessed: 25 February 2008).

Motion Picture Association of America (2006a) 'MPAA releases data from piracy study', press release; available at: *www.mpaa.org/press_releases/2006_05_03lek.pdf* (accessed: 8 January 2008).

Motion Picture Association of America (2006b) 'Respect copyrights: curriculum for the Los Angeles Boy Scouts of America', press release; available at: *www.mpaa.org/press_ releases/RespectCopyrightsCurriculum.pdf* (accessed: 25 February 2008).

Norgaard, Rolf (2004) 'Writing information literacy in the classroom: pedagogical enactments and implications', *Reference & User Services Quarterly*, 43(3): 220–6.

Park, Chris (2004) 'Rebels without a clause: towards an institutional framework for dealing with plagiarism by students', *Journal of Further and Higher Education*, 28(3): 291–306.

Patinkin, Mark (2006) 'How Kaavya Viswanathan got herself packaged', *Providence Journal*, 9 May; available at: *kaavya-viswanathan-news.newslib.com/story/8246- 58/* (accessed: 25 February 2008).

Peterson, Lorna (1998) 'Teaching academic integrity: opportunities in bibliographic instruction', *Research Strategies*, 6(4): 168–76.

Pennycook, A. (1996) 'Borrowing others' words: text, ownership, memory and plagiarism', *TESOL Quarterly*,

30(2): 201–30.

Pierson, David (2006) 'A merit badge that can't be duplicated; MPAA, Scouts team up to offer an anti-piracy award but will youths who see downloading as harmless strive for this patch?', *Los Angeles Times*, 21 October, p. B1.

Pincus, Holly Seirup and Schmelkin, Liora Pedhazur (2003) 'Faculty perceptions of academic dishonesty: a multidimensional scaling analysis', *Journal of Higher Education*, 74(2): 196–209.

Pino, Nathan W. and Smith, William L. (2003) 'College students and academic dishonesty', *College Student Journal*, 37(4): 490–500.

Plum, Stephen (1984) 'Library use and the development of critical thought', in Thomas G. Kirk Jr (ed.) *Increasing the Teaching Roles of Academic Libraries in New Directions for Teaching and Learning*, New Directions for Teaching and Learning No. 18. San Francisco: Jossey-Bass, pp. 25–33.

Posner, Richard (2007) *The Little Book of Plagiarism*. New York: Pantheon Books.

Ramsay, Karen M. and Kinnie, Jim (2006) 'The embedded librarian: getting out there via technology to help students where they learn', *Library Journal*, 131(6): 34–5.

Random House (2006) 'Random House calls sophomore's response deeply troubling and disingenuous', press release, 28 April; available at: *www.randomhouse.biz/media/publicity* (accessed: 25 February 2008).

Raspa, Richard and Ward, Dane (eds) (2000) *The Collaborative Imperative: Librarians and Faculty Working Together in the Information Universe*. Chicago: ACRL.

Rawe, Julie (2007) 'A question of honor', *Time Magazine*, 169(22): 59.

Rivlin, Harry N. (1942) 'The writing of term papers', *Journal of Higher Education*, 13(6): 314, 320–42.

Robbins, Alexandra (2006) *The Overachievers: The Secret Lives of Driven Kids*. New York: Hyperion Press.

Robinson, Jennifer (1992) 'International students and American university culture: adjustment issues', paper presented at Washington Area Teachers of English to Speakers of Other Languages (WATESOL) Annual Convention, Arlington, VA, 16 October, ERIC Document ED350968.

Rockman, Ilene F. (2004) *Integrating Information Literacy into the Higher Education Curriculum: Practical Models for Transformation*, Jossey-Bass Higher and Adult Education Series. San Francisco: Jossey-Bass.

Roth, Lorie (1999) 'Educating the cut-and-paste generation', *Library Journal*, 124(18): 42–4.

Royce, John (2003) 'Has Turnitin.com got it all wrapped up?', *Teacher Librarian*, 30(4): 26–31.

Rutgers (2003) 'New study confirms internet plagiarism is prevalent', *News*, State University of New Jersey, 28 August; available at: *http://ur.rutgers.edu/medrel/ viewArticle.html?ArticleID=3408* (accessed: 25 February 2008).

Saint Louis University Libraries (2007) 'Pius library news blog'; available at: *http://puislibrarynews.wordpress .com/2007/08/20/writing-center-opens-new-location-in-pius-library* (accessed: 25 February 2008).

Scanlon, Patrick (2003) 'Student online plagiarism: how do we respond?', *College Teaching*, 51(4): 161–5.

Schleicher, Annie (2006) 'Plagiarism scandal exposes world of book packaging', cited 10 January 2008; available at: *www.pbs.org/newshour/extra/features/jan-june06/ author_5-03.html* (accessed: 25 February 2008).

Scollon, R. (1995) 'Plagiarism and ideology: identity in

intercultural discourse', *Language in Society*, 24(1): 1–28.

Shanbhag, Shilpa (2007) 'Door-in-the-face: understandings of scholarship for academic instruction librarians', *Library Philosophy and Practice*, June; available at: *www.webpages.uidaho.edu/~mbolin/shanbhag2.pdf* (accessed: 25 February 2008).

Sheridan, Jean (ed.) (1995) *Writing-Across-the-Curriculum and the Academic Library: A Guide for Librarians, Instructors, and Writing Program Directors*. Westport, CT: Greenwood Press.

Simmons, Michelle Holschuh (2005) 'Librarians as disciplinary discourse mediators: using genre theory to move toward critical information literacy', *Portal: Libraries and the Academy*, 5(3): 297–311.

Sisti, Dominic (2007) 'How do high school students justify internet plagiarism?', *Ethics & Behavior*, 17(3): 215–31.

Smalley, Topsy and Plum, Stephen (1982) 'Teaching library research in the humanities and the sciences', in Cerise Oberman and Katrina Strauch (eds) *Theories of Bibliographic Instruction: Designs for Teaching*. New York and London: R.R. Bowker, pp. 135–70.

Snapper, John (1999) 'On the web, plagiarism matters more than copyright piracy', *Ethics and Information Technology*, 1(2): 127–35.

Staff and Agencies (2004) 'Plagiarising student sues university for negligence', *Guardian UK*, 27 May; available at: *http://education.guardian.co.uk/higher/news/story/0,,1226148,00.html* (accessed: 25 February 2008).

Stepchyshyn, Vera and Nelson, Robert S. (eds) (2007) *Library Plagiarism Policies*, College Library Information Packet No. 37 (CLIP Note). Chicago: ACRL.

Swan, J.C. (1982) 'Ethics at the reference desk: comfortable theories and tricky practices', *Reference Librarian*, 4:

99–106.

Swartz, Pauline, Carlisle, Brian and Uyeki, E. Chisato (2007) 'Librarians and student affairs: partners for student success', *Reference Services Review*, 35(1): 109–22.

Sydney Morning Herald (2006) 'YouTube to make life even busier for Google lawyers', *Sydney Morning Herald*, 23 October; available at: *www.smh.com.au/news/ business/youtube-to-make-life-even-busier-for-google- lawyers/2006/10/23/1161455662458.html?page=1* (accessed: 26 February 2008).

Tomaiuolo, Nicholas (2007) 'Citations and aberrations', *Searcher Magazine*, July/August, p. 17.

Trussell, Alice (2004) 'Librarians and engineering faculty: partnerships and opportunities in information literacy and ethics instruction'; available at: *www.iatul.org/ doclibrary/public/Conf_Proceedings/2004/Alice20Trussel l.pdf* (accessed: 26 February 2008).

Turnitin.com (2007) 'About us'; available at: *http:// Turnitin.com/static/company.html* (accessed: 26 February 2008).

University of California Los Angeles Libraries (2007) 'Citations 101 workshop outline'; available at: *http://staff.library.ucla.edu/newsweb1040.htm* (accessed: 26 February 2008).

University of Connecticut Libraries (2007) 'Academic liaison program'; available at: *www.lib.uconn.edu/using/ services/liaison/prog00.htm* (accessed: 26 February 2008).

University of Kansas Writing Center (2007) 'Addressing plagiarism: KU writing center'; available at: *www.writing.ku.edu/instructors/docs/plagiarism1.shtml* (accessed: 26 February 2008).

Van Cleave, Kendra (2007) 'Collaboration', in Susan Curzon and Lynn Lampert (eds) *Proven Strategies for*

Building an Information Literacy Program. New York: Neal Schuman, pp. 177–90.

Volokh, Eugene (2006) 'Plagiarism and "atonement"', *Wall Street Journal (Europe)*, 12 December, p. 14.

Walker, John (1998) 'Student plagiarism in universities: what are we doing about it?', *Higher Education Research & Development*, 17(1): 89–106.

Walker, Teresa, Row, Jane S. and Dolence, Travis (2007) 'Teaching and supporting EndNote at the University of Tennessee: designing online alternatives to high demand classes', *Electronic Journal of Academic and Special Librarianship*, 8(2); available at: *http:// southernlibrarianship.icaap.org/content/v08n02/walker_t01 .html* (accessed: 26 February 2008).

Walter, Scott (2006) 'Outreach to student services', paper presented at Annual Meeting of the American Library Association, New Orleans, 22–28 June.

Walter, Scott and Eodice, Michelle (2007) 'Meeting the student learning imperative: supporting and sustaining collaboration between academic libraries and student', *Research Strategies*, 20(4): 219–25.

Wang, Li (2008) 'Sociocultural learning theories and information literacy teaching activities in higher education', *Reference & User Services Quarterly*, 47(2): 149–58.

Whitley, Bernard E. and Keith-Spiegel, Patricia (2002) *Academic Dishonesty: An Educator's Guide*. Mahwah, NJ: Lawrence Erlbaum.

Willmott, Chris J.R. and Harrison, Tim M. (2003) 'An exercise to teach bioscience students about plagiarism', *Journal of Biological Education*, 37(3): 139–41.

Young, Lauren (2004) 'Internet takes blame for increase in cheating, University of California Santa Barbara', *Daily Nexus*, 28 May; available at: *www.dailynexus.com/*

article.php?a=7703 (accessed: 26 February 2008).

YouTube.com (2007) 'YouTube – broadcast yourself'; available at: *www.youtube.com/t/howto_copyright* (accessed: 2 February 2007).

Zeller, Tom Jr (2006) 'A guest blogger, and an unwritten law', *New York Times*, 20 March; available at: *www.nytimes.com/2006/03/20/business/20link.html?_r= 1&oref=slogin* (accessed: 25 February 2008).

Further reading

Associated Press (2006) 'This piracy patch isn't worn over the eye, Scout's honor', *Chicago Tribune*, 22 October, p. 3.

Bradicals and Tarquinn (2007) *RefWorks: The Ultimate Tool for Bibliographies*, video, Arizona State University Libraries; available at: *www.youtube.com/watch?v= OMFTvX%PqQ8* and *http://univids.com/video/ refworks-ultimate-tool-bibliographies* (accessed: 26 February 2008).

Bucknell University (2007) 'Students – RefWorks can help you format your citations correctly'; available at: *http://blogs.bucknell.edu/isr/2007/03/students_refworks_ can_help_you.html* (accessed: 26 February 2008).

Citation Machine (2008) 'Citation Machine'; available at: *http://citationmachine.net/* (accessed: 26 February 2008).

Colorado State University (2007) 'RefWorks for students workshop'; available at: *http://csuplibrary.wordpress. com/2007/04/16/refworks-for-students-workshop/* (accessed: 26 February 2008).

Curzon, Susan C. and Lampert, Lynn D. (eds) (2007) *Proven Strategies for Building an Information Literacy Program*. New York: Neal Schuman.

Dalhousie University Library (2008) 'RefWorks workshops'; available at: *www.library.dal.ca/How/*

Classes/Killam (accessed: 26 February 2008).

Earle, Toby (2004) 'Internet plagiarizing student sues university', *WebUser*, 28 May; available at: *www.webuser.co.uk/news/49305.html* (accessed: 26 February 2008).

Gentile, Gary (2006) 'Yes there's a patch for that: Scouts encouraged to fight piracy', *Daily Breeze*, 22 October, p. A1.

Marsalis, Scott and Kelley, Julia (2004) 'Building a RefWorks database of faculty publications as a liaison and collection development tool', *Issues in Science & Technology Librarianship*, 40 (Summer); available at: *www.istl.org/04-summer/article3.html* (accessed: 26 February 2008).

McCabe, Donald L. and Trevino, Linda Klebe (2002) 'Honesty and honor codes', *Academe*, 881: 37–41.

McCabe, Donald L., Butterfield, Kenneth D. and Trevino, Linda Klebe (2001) 'Cheating in academic institutions: a decade of research', *Ethics & Behavior*, 11(3): 219–32.

NoodleTools.com (2008) 'NoodleBib'; available at: *www.noodlebib.com* (accessed: 26 February 2008).

San Diego State University (2007) 'RefWorks @ SDSU'; available at: *http://infodome.sdsu.edu/refworks/index.shtml* (accessed: 26 February 2008).

State University of New York at Plattsburgh (2007) 'Preventing and detecting plagiarism: a faculty workshop'; available at: *http://faculty.plattsburgh.edu/holly.hellerross/Plagiarism.htm* (accessed: 26 February 2008).

Tufts University Library (2007) 'Research paper navigator learning module'; available at: *www.library.tufts.edu/researchpaper/* (accessed: 26 February 2008).

University of California Los Angeles Libraries (2006) *Carlos and Eddie's Guide to Bruin Success with Less*

Stress, tutorial; available at: *www.library.ucla.edu/bruinsuccess* (accessed: 26 February 2008).

University of Maine, Farmington (2007) 'Synthesis: using the work of others', available at: *http://plagiarism.umf.maine.edu* (accessed: 26 February 2008).

University of North Carolina at Chapel Hill Libraries (2007) 'International student library tutorial'; available at: *www.lib.unc.edu/instruct/international/index.html* (accessed: 26 February 2008).

White, Edward M. (1993) 'Too many campuses want to sweep student plagiarism under the rug', *Chronicle of Higher Education*, 24 February, p. A44.

Index